DIEGO MARADONA

DIEGO MARADONA
THE LAST INTERVIEW
and OTHER CONVERSATIONS

with an introduction by ROGER BENNETT

MELVILLE HOUSE
BROOKLYN • LONDON

CONTENTS

INTRODUCTION

ROGER BENNETT

One of Diego Armando Maradona's most remarkable legacies is that the tiny giant provided everyone blessed to have watched him play with some of their most profound life memories. I am among them. As a kid growing up in Liverpool, Maradona's single-handed 1986 World Cup destruction of the England national football team by means most foul, was one of the most brutal life lessons I learned in my teens: a crash course in ethics. The game, played at the Estadio Azteca in Mexico City, in the shadow of the 1982 Falklands War, saw "El Pibe de Oro" score two of the most unforgettable World Cup goals of all time. One illegitimate, in which the squat five-foot-five-inch Diego used his left fist to reach over a six-foot goalkeeper and punch the ball into the net—an arch moment of impudence which became known as "The Hand of God" as soon as the Argentinian admitted it had been scored "a little with the head of Maradona and a little with the hand of God." Four minutes later, while the English were still reeling, he scored a solo goal even God would have had problems replicating, lacerating the entire English team in the course of a spectacular sixty-yard dash, during which he slalomed through six English players while, in the words of the British commentator, "turning like a little eel."

This was an English team that prided itself on grit and physicality. The last two defenders attempted to take out the man rather than the ball, only to bounce off him. I still swear you could hear Maradona's scornful laughter as they did so. So breathtaking was the goal that Steve Hodge, the English midfielder charged with marking Maradona, revealed that his impulse as the ball crossed the line was to clap. I felt far less charitable in the moment, experiencing my heroes' emasculation as failure. Seething with rage at the final whistle, my brother and I charged outside, desperate for the kind of emotional release that can only be gained by playing football in the street.

Overwhelmed by grief, and desperate to vent, I blasted the first shot that came my way straight through the window of our home. Before the shattered glass had finished falling from the window, my father came outside to find me standing in the middle of the road with tears of anger still stinging. Rather than being annoyed, my father shared our pain. He simply nodded, then solemnly hugged us both. "I understand, lads," he said. "I understand."

Over time, my perspective on football—like that on beer, Jell-O, and leafy greens—has evolved. I have come to realize that football's greatest gift is its ability to make you feel. I often joke that the sport allows me to experience human emotions, such as joy, misery, victory, and loss, that normal people experience in real life but that I am dead to inside. No one made me feel more alive than Maradona in that moment, and I am not alone. Throughout his career, Maradona made entire cities, regions, and nations come together and share some of the most profound, empowering, and joyful experiences of their lives.

Cherubic of face, curly of hair, Diego rose to become a religious icon. There is a line in Asif Kapadia's incredible film *Diego Maradona* in which it is revealed that almost every home in Naples had a photo of Maradona hanging on a wall, many alongside an image of Jesus. I once corresponded with the late Uruguayan poet Eduardo Galeano and asked him about his warning in relation to Maradona: "When humans become gods, there is only one ultimate outcome, they have to become fallen gods." Anyone who watched Maradona flail during the embers of his career will know this is true—even more so throughout his peripatetic retirement in which he often cut a beleaguered, corpulent figure in search of sanctuary.

Galeano explained: "Maradona became a kind of dirty god, the most human of the gods. That perhaps explains the universal veneration he conquered, more than any other player." I love that framing: the most human of gods. A gent who experienced extremes of ecstasy and misery, veneration and loneliness, in a way that encapsulates life itself. Shortly after my conversation with Galeano, I came into possession of a signed photograph of Maradona punching the ball over Peter Shilton, the bewildered England goalkeeper. I framed the image and hung it on the wall opposite my desk, where it sits today. A moment which traumatized me so badly as a kid is now the one thing I look at every single day—a reminder of Diego, his power, and his singular ability to make the world feel alive.

DIEGO MARADONA

THE FIRST INTERVIEW

INTERVIEW BY TITO BIONDI
SABADOS CIRCULARES
1972

BIONDI: What are your dreams?

MARADONA: I have two dreams. My first dream is to play in the World Cup. The second is to be champion of the quarter-finals and what comes next of this season [with Argentinos Juniors].*

---

* A twelve-year-old Maradona was interviewed for a children's television program. He was filmed in what looked like a paddock, wearing a number 10 shirt, juggling a ball with with absolute ease. This interview—or a slice of it—went into heavy rotation when Maradona led Argentina to victory in the 1986 World Cup. The interview was invested with prophetic power, but he was misquoted in saying, "I have two dreams. My first dream is to play in the World Cup. And the second dream is to win it." Maradona's ambitions were a little more prosaic. He did express a desire to play in the World Cup, but the championship he had his mind on was the championship that his youth team, Argentinos Juniors–also know as Las Cebollitas— was involved in.

THE DAY MARADONA MET PELÉ

INTERVIEW BY GUILLERMO BLANCO
EL GRÁFICO
1979
TRANSLATED BY MARISSA COLON-MARGOLIES

Pelé has put down his guitar and is giving Diego advice. They take each other's hands. Diego's tremulous and emotional; Pelé's calm and gentle. I see in Maradona's eyes how he defers to Pelé and becomes emotional when the king takes off his crown and shows how humble and sincere he can be, when he shows a side of himself that is rarely seen. How long has it been since Pelé has had a moment to laugh, sing, relax or speak about whatever he wants? He's always traveling (in less than an hour he'll fly to Santos), always signing business deals, divorce agreements, purchases, sales, films, recordings, reports, always going, coming back, never there.

Because of this, the astonished dark-haired friend who observes him, will later assure others that he's never seen Pelé like this, so open and spontaneous, so giving and happy, so Edson Arantes do Nascimento as God made him. Because of this, these clasped hands summarize everything. Pelé speaks in the softly rough voice he uses every morning and forgets the demands of the present moment in order to give advice to Diego. And Diego still can't believe that he's there side by side with Pelé like he's dreamed all his life—and like he's going to dream afterwards.

How many freezing nights in Villa Fiorito have you, Maradona, spent imagining that you were playing one-twos with Pelé? How many times have you suddenly woken up and pinched yourself, thinking, "What the heck am I dreaming about if I'm never going to get closer than 100 meters to him to ask for an autograph?" Now, Diego, you have the ball and the shirt from the Brazilian national team that Pelé signed five minutes ago. You have a medal with a chain that you will keep all your life like a war trophy. And you will bring Lato or Hugo, your two younger brothers, the watch that Pelé will give you during this chat. But beyond all of this are these joined hands to which we will have to return to discover the root of things. Pelé speaking as if he were the father, Pelé speaking to Maradona and seeing in him his brother Foca, whom in Santos they wanted to transform into another Pelé, but were unable to because Foca refused, saying "There's only one Pelé."

MARADONA: Please, what sacrifice? No, no. I've wanted to meet you for a really long time . . .

PELÉ: You didn't have to come all this way, we're all the same here.

And he continues with his advice, mixing in a smile, a pleased look for those of us on this twelfth floor of the 1782 Avenida Atlantica building next to Copacabana Beach in Río.

PELÉ: It angers me that I have to go. Because I didn't think you were going to come all the way here after the game yesterday, I arranged with my lawyer Samir to go to Santos to work on some paperwork, taxes and tax returns, you understand?

And now I'd like to stay and have lunch with you. Tell me, how is your team doing, eh?

MARADONA: We're in first place, we've been having a good season. Delem is our coach; he sends you his best.

PELÉ: Ah, yes, Delem! A really good guy. So you're in first place?

MARADONA: Yes, Pelé. Yesterday we beat Huracán 3–1; we scored some beautiful goals and the hinchada [hardcore fans] are following us everywhere.

PELÉ: That's great, Diego. Look, Maradona will not have to come to Río anymore to see Pelé. I promise you that if your team Argentinos gets to the finals of the championship in Buenos Aires, I will go to Argentina to see you, OK? I was worried yesterday because I knew that if you came, I wasn't going to be able to receive you like I would have wanted to due to scheduling issues. I don't even have a gift for you . . . but wait a minute, I'll be back . . .

He doesn't send anyone, as would be logical, given his status. A detail that confirms his transformation. He goes down the stairs and in a few minutes will be back. Down there, on the balcony with the whole view of the river, is the owner of the house. Alfredo Saad. He's a Brazilian business man who usually has the Khaled Princes from Saudi Arabia as his guests, old friends with whom he organized the transfer of Roberto Rivelino to the Arab football league.

Saad had a bed made for when Pelé is in Rió valued at a million cruzeiros (30,000 dollars.) He constructed a helipad to facilitate rapid access from any location: from there above Pelé comes and goes whenever he needs. Three Brazilian presidents have lived in the Chopin Building (where we are): Cáfe Filho, Joao Goulart and Juscelino Kubístchek. At the front desk there is a special security guard who restricts access to anyone who isn't authorized to enter. This man [Saad] speaks with the Maradona party and he gives them what almost sounds like an order—"You guys already know this. When you want to come to Río call me and come stay in my house. You will be my honored guests."

Surely, he will offer them one of his three Rolls Royces to use, his forty-six-foot yacht or the white Cadillac that is now sitting outside the door of the building. And if Diego wants to train, he'll also be offered the use of the pull-up bars, the stationary bicycle, the mats and the rest of the equipment that sits in a training room. This is Pelé's home in Río. This is the place where Diego Armando Maradona, together with his father and his friend and agent Jorge Cyterszpiler, go along with *El Gráfico* after days of difficult coordination, sacrifice and the stories they'll always remember, while Pelé looks unflaggingly for a pair of presents to give to Diego.

The operation began at the end of January on the beaches of Atlántida, Uruguay. Diego's confession kicked it all off: "I'm dying to meet Pelé."

From then on, a series of actions began—the largest impediment was Pelé's lack of time—and extended from New York to Santos and Río, and culminated in this affectionate and sincere meeting.

Eventually, *El Gráfico* spoke with Diego and gave him the good news. We can see Pelé Friday morning. But Maradona is conscious of the fact that the national team is more important than any personal desire of his, and says he prefers to stay and train in San Isidro. Saturday a telex from our man in Río notifies us that Pelé can receive Diego on Monday morning. But there is an insurmountable hurdle: getting Diego, his father and his agent to board British Caledonian Flight 664 on Sunday at 7:30 p.m., an improbable feat, given that Argentinos Juniors are set to finish playing Huracán at 5:45 p.m., and they would have to get to Ezeiza airport by 6:30 p.m. Starting at 3:00 p.m., two taxis are waiting, ready at the stadium door to drive them over at the right moment.

El Gráfico was already at the locker-room door to ensure the effectiveness of the operation so that the player could leave as quickly as possible. The president of the soccer club, Próspero Consoli, informed about the trip by a third party, tried to impose his authority:

CONSOLI: Diego, where are you hurrying off to?

MARADONA: To Brazil.

CONSOLI: Who gave you permission, eh?

MARADONA: Ah just a moment. Eh? Starting right now, I no longer belong to Argentinos Juniors. Starting now, I belong to the national team, and because I'm thinking of going to train and stay at José C. Paz [the national team's training grounds], I'm not worried.

Some people on the plane have nothing to do with soccer, but others do. Like the young person who discovers Maradona and, stunned, begins a rumor: "Look, that's Maradona, they've already sold him to Barcelona," the man says without realizing that the plane isn't headed to Spain.

Another asked where he was going and after receiving an answer, investigated further: "And to which Brazilian club did they sell you to?"

In first class, four seats waited for them with glasses full of champagne. There, they made the first toast for everything to turn out well and for Diego to be able to meet Pelé, "one of the highest aspirations of my life."

MARADONA: I don't know; I'd settle for him giving me, I don't know, five, ten minutes. I've heard that he's a very busy man with lots of problems and because of this he might not even be able to meet with us; but I still think it was worth the effort to make this trip. Everything hurts, I swear. I have a huge bruise because Bábington kicked my leg in the first half. Afterwards it was hard for me to run. I even told Delem that I couldn't keep playing, but he didn't let me leave the field. My shoulder also hurts. I'm going to see if I can sleep a little, and when we get to the hotel I'll put some ice on my leg.

Maradona's dad doesn't say anything. He's staring into space and doesn't hear when people speak to him. "Pelé is going to welcome Pelusa. My God," he will be thinking.

Diego's agent and friend, Jorge, is thinking about whether he can make some sort of deal with Pelé. But he doesn't stop going over Diego's contract, which he'll have to fight for as soon as they return to Buenos Aires. Jorge has accompanied Maradona since the era in which Diego got to Cebollitas de la Paternal. He looks like a kid; like Diego, he's twenty years old, but when Maradona's interests need defending, he's the first to stand up.

Are you Maradona? They ask him in Portugese when he steps onto Brazilian soil. He's going incognito so he doesn't answer. Neither yes or no. The Copacabana Palace hotel is waiting with all its history in tow. In homage to this hotel, Julio de Caro composed the tango "Copacabana" in the 1930s. Fifty meters away, on the same block, is the building where one finds Pelé. It's past midnight. It's time to eat and relax because at eleven in the morning the next day, Pelé will be waiting.

MARADONA: I swear it'll be just ten minutes and I'm gonna feel immortal, like I'm [Carlos] Gardel [the father of the tango].

Diego was far from believing that the next day, Pelé would receive him with open arms, a huge smile, sincerity shining on his face, a yellow shirt embroidered with white flowers, white pants, white sandals, a very fine gold watch—the clothing he's wearing now when he returns from downstairs and says to Maradona:

PELÉ: I'm sorry Diego that I don't have more to give you. Do you have siblings?

MARADONA: Yes, there are eight of us: five sisters and three brothers.

PELÉ: Ehh Papá! [Pelé laughs, looking at Maradona's dad.]

MARADONA: Pelé, seriously, don't worry about us, you don't have to bother.

PELÉ: But it's not a bother at all. I have this watch, it's not good, it can't get wet, what am I going to do with it? Give it as a gift to one of your brothers, and this medal is for you. It was made for my farewell game at Cosmos.

MARADONA: Thank you so much, I am going to keep it for the rest of my life. I saw your game on Friday on TV and I swear it made me really emotional and made me want to see you even more.

PELÉ: Honestly, I got emotional on Friday too. The stadium was like a frying pan with 170,000 people and me again in the middle of it. It was a really special feeling to know that the people still love me, that they remember me. Flamengo plays good football. They adapted to me. They pass the ball so that I could play almost standing still, you know what I mean? Eh? Shooting balls. I'm trained to always run, but as you get older the years weigh on you.

MARADONA: I wanted you to keep playing in the second half.

PELÉ: Forty-five minutes was enough. I hadn't practiced nearly at all with the team. Thursday there were like ten thousand people at practice. [*pause*] Diego, I'm really happy to have met you.

MARADONA: And I don't even have the words.

PELÉ: Say hello to Delem for me and tell him good luck.

The lawyer is watching. He wants to leave for Santos. The driver Alfredo is waiting too. Pelé continues in this world that once belonged to him. Even the wrinkles on Diego's dad's face make Pelé remember his own father.

The guitar is now on the table. Pelé barely played any chords during the visit. "I can't sing, I've lost my voice. You know? I just recorded a record for kids to support International Children's Day. I like writing songs. I also like kids."

MARADONA: Pelé, are you going to play any other games I could see? Because I only saw you play against Huracán in Buenos Aires. Do you remember that game?

PELÉ: Yes, I think that was my last game in Argentina. Look, I'm going to play charity games often. I think I can be useful to many organizations and people in need, you know? [*The lawyer gives Pelé a look that shows he is inflexible (their time is up). Pelé gives up and stands.*]

Papá [*he turns to Maradona's dad*], take care of the kid, OK? [*Don Diego nods and gives him a hug.*] Diego, I hope God gives you all the luck that he gave me, and that like me, you never get knocked down.

MARADONA: Thank you Pelé.

Now the hugs finish. We're in the elevator and soon we will be back in Buenos Aires. It felt like a century. It was an hour. I ask him: What can you tell me?

MARADONA: I knew that as a player, he was a god; now I know he's also one as a person. He's Pelé for a reason. How many kids like me want to see him, touch him, exchange a few words, and I had the privilege, he even gave me advice. I saw that Pelé was coming towards me and I couldn't believe it. Because we were waiting and he was the one that came and gave me a hug and a hug to my dad, and he called my old man "dad." When we were talking I felt like he was doting on me. I grabbed his hand and was left feeling stunned. I had asked two things of Christ the Redeemer the night before, when we arrived. I'm not going to tell you what. I saw how my father cried when Pelé gave me advice. To have met Pelé is like the World Cup that I never had. Not more or less. Now I want to tell everyone everything. Tell Delem and my Argentinian compañeros and everyone from the national team, everyone in the world.

Maradona will continue to rush through his chosen world. You, Diego Armando Maradona, cementing your own destiny, dribbling and dodging as you move forward. But you'll go forward with an advantage, you're taking with you the advice Pelé gave you on Monday, April 9, 1979, a sunny day, under a blue sky in Copacabana:

PELÉ: Don't listen when they tell you you're the best. You should never think you're best. The day you think you're the best, you'll stop being serious forever.

Accept the applause, but don't live for the applause. At eighteen years old, I got whistled at a lot. The fans start yelling at you after three games when you play badly, they stop loving you.

I want to tell you something about contracts. Every player has his own problem. It's a personal issue, but keep in mind that you have to fight for what you're really worth. Demand respect, never give yourself away, but if you sign a contract, later, don't ask for more. A signature is like giving your word.

With respect to playing abroad, make a decision after you've analyzed things carefully. You've told me that you have eight siblings, your mom and dad. When it's time to make a decision, weigh this as well. The club managers change every two or three years. You have to think about your family because there are a lot of mouths to feed.

Your physical condition is the tool with which you do your work. From what I can see, you are in very good shape. Take care of your body. In life, there is time for everything, even if you are a soccer player. There's time to go out, to have a drink, to smoke a cigarette, to go to sleep late, to eat the food that you like. But do it in a balanced way. Always do what doesn't hurt your physical condition, otherwise, all of this will end. Would you like to play in the United States? No, it's a joke to make you laugh. You still have a lot to give. There is good money there. They pay for twelve months and you only pay for five. But wait, wait, you have a lot of time ahead of you . . .

ON HIS WAY TO WEMBLEY

INTERVIEW WITH REX GOWAR
UNPUBLISHED INTERVIEW*
APRIL 1980

* *A portion of this unpublished interview was intended to run in* Shoot *magazine in London, but a printers' strike resulted in the issue never going to press.*

Diego Maradona took on half the England team in the 1986 World Cup quarterfinals and beat them to score a magnificent goal, and he did the same twice against Belgium in the semifinals.

He was taking on and overcoming such challenges six, seven years earlier every weekend when he was still a raw "pibe"—"kid" in Argentine slang—playing for Argentinos Juniors.

Among his victims then were Ubaldo Fillol, River Plate's 1978 World Cup–winning goalkeeper, who fell for the kind of dummy Pelé sold Uruguay's Lasdislao Mazurkiewicz in the 1970 World Cup, and Hugo Gatti of Boca Juniors.

Gatti once called Maradona a fatty in the buildup to a match between Boca and Argentinos Juniors. Maradona promised to put a hat trick past Gatti and ended up beating him four times: from open play, in a counterattack, from a penalty, and with a free kick from close to the corner flag, which he curled inside the top far corner of Gatti's net.

Headlines that included the words "Maradona" and "magic" became commonplace; he beat Brazil's Leao with a brilliant curling shot for Argentina against the rest of the world in Buenos Aires, and we watched on television as he beat Scotland's Alan Rough with a cheeky first goal for his country in Glasgow in 1979.

That was after inspiring Argentina to victory in the 1979 World Youth Cup in Japan. Millions of Argentines stayed up at night to watch that tournament, featuring one of the country's most popular teams ever.

A year later Maradona had a Wembley crowd on the edge of their seats with a run that nearly delivered a goal similar to his second against England in Mexico City in 1986.

MARADONA MAGIC

The consensus among Argentine football followers in the late 1970s was that we should try to see Maradona in action as often as possible before this gem of a player was whisked away by a rich European club.

The world saw what Maradona was capable of doing with a football during his peak years with Napoli and captaining Argentina to World Cup victory in Mexico in 1986. What we saw on pitches around Buenos Aires, from River Plate's Monumental stadium to the ten-thousand-capacity ground with wooden terracing of the Asociación Atlética Argentinos Juniors, a modest club with a very successful scouting system, was equally eye-popping.

Maradona had the country in thrall: the old timers because he reminded them of Argentina's first golden era in the 1940s when, they said, every team had three Maradonas, and the young because he was magical.

Going to matches then as a photographer for an Argentine newspaper, I regularly saw Maradona play in his teens and covered the efforts of Argentinos Juniors to hang onto their gem, to the extent of having him declared a national treasure, and his move across town to Boca Juniors in 1981 when he was twenty.

FIRST AGENT

Maradona gave me an exclusive interview as a nineteen-year-old in April 1980, weeks before playing for the first time against England at Wembley on a European tour by then world champions Argentina.

Even then, he already had a team of people looking after his affairs, headed by his first personal agent, his neighbour Jorge Cyterszpiler in the middle-class barrio where Maradona moved his family from the Villa Fiorito shanty town of his birth with his first big bucks.

In one of many contrasts that were to mark Maradona's life, the ultimate footballing genius was represented by a clever kid of the same age with economic qualifications, who had been struck down by polio in childhood.

I had to go and see Cyterszpiler three times at a small first-floor office on a narrow downtown street in Buenos Aires before getting the interview at a hotel in a western barrio where Argentinos Juniors concentrated before home matches.

The ambition was there from the beginning, along with a certain teenage modesty.

Maradona had his critics but their voice was as nothing amid the idolatry of the crowds for the country's most popular figure since Eva Peron . . . and like Evita, he delivered, brilliantly, memorably, controversially.

Not everyone liked his lavish, celebrity lifestyle, his friends, many of them hangers-on, his over-the-top wedding to girl-next-door sweetheart Claudia Villafañe, but Argentines overlooked all of this because with Maradona, Argentina was always tipped to win.

GOWAR: You're going to England for the first time. What are your thoughts about the game there?

MARADONA: I think the biggest thing is to play in that stadium, right? I think it's the best field to play football that there is in the world. And to play in England I think is important because lately I think they have one of the best national teams in the world.

GOWAR: The other day England beat Spain in Spain, playing quite well.

MARADONA: Yes, and [Kevin] Keegan is a superb player whom I like a lot. Let's see what happens because we're very well prepared to be able to beat England.

GOWAR: What does Argentina expect from this match and the tour?

MARADONA: Argentina can no longer go to speculate, because we can no longer go looking for the little point to look good. Argentina is working with a right the team has earned and can't get fixated on defending or anything like that because in Spain [at the 1982 World Cup] we're going to have to win all our matches, so César [Menotti] will send us out to attack while being careful.

GOWAR: What do you recall of previous matches between Argentina and England? For example the one that was played here (a 1–1 draw in Buenos Aires in June 1977) several years ago? Were you in the squad?

MARADONA: No, but I went to see the game. I didn't like it much, to be sincere. England came to defend, to avoid a poor show, and Argentina wasn't playing well then either, so it turned into a very poor match with most of the action in the middle of the field; there was a lot of running but no ideas.

GOWAR: What do you know about Keegan?

MARADONA: I've seen him play [for Hamburg] in German matches they show here in Argentina [on TV] and I really like the style of game he has, he's everywhere, and I also saw him score some great goals; it's obvious he's a phenomenal player. Now he's moving to a small English team [Southampton].

GOWAR: It's a small club with ambitions of becoming bigger. [Mick] Channon, who also played in the [1977] draw here, is at that club.

MARADONA: Argentina are not going to go looking for a result but rather to play thinking of 1982.

GOWAR: Last year you were also on the tour, your first. Do you feel more confident in how well you can play?

MARADONA: I have the same motivations, the same hopes I had before; I'm not going to pretend I'm neither calmer nor more desperate for this tour. I want to go out onto the pitch and hope they all pass me the ball, right? Because the day I lose my motivation for going out onto the field I could give my rivals an advantage.

GOWAR: And as for how well the team can play given that two years have passed since the World Cup? Will there be more changes in the team?

MARADONA: There were a couple of changes, but I don't think much changed; the players who left [to play overseas] were very important, like [Osvaldo] Ardiles, but we have [Juan] Barbas who replaced him very well in the game with Scotland and he also came on against Holland so there's not much difference.

GOWAR: Which players in the national team will make a good impression in the match against England?

MARADONA: I don't know how Argentina will line up but [Carlos] Fren, who is a very good [midfield] player, has come [into the squad], also [Carlos] Ischia who is new in the team and in good form, so they are going to be at the same level as all those who have already played. I think César chooses very well.

GOWAR: What influence has Menotti had on your career?

MARADONA: He is very important because, aside from giving me the chance to play for the national team, he's always giving me advice before each game and in training. And I think part of my success is thanks to him.

GOWAR: What did it mean to you to win the Youth World Cup [in Japan in 1979]?

MARADONA: It's the biggest thing in my life because I had never won a championship like that as a professional, and to show what Argentine football is like with all the other teams in the world and beat them well, not with ease but with clarity, showing what Argentine football has with its passing game, rotating and reaching the goal.

GOWAR: Is Menotti right not to use the exiles on tour, those who are [with clubs] in Europe, especially [Ricardo] Villa and Ardiles,* in the match against England?

MARADONA: They are national team players, for instance Ardiles whom I personally like very much, but César says he wants to play with the players he has here at hand. I think that's okay, but I don't rule out the possibility that for the '82 World Cup the players that can be good for the national team will be there, who have more experience than those here and fundamentally play a different game and can be very important.

---

* Ardiles and Villa moved to Tottenham Hotspur in 1979 and proceeded to become club legends there.

GOWAR: What does England mean to you in football terms?

MARADONA: I've been told a lot about England; [Alberto] Tarantini is always talking about it, and they say lots of people go to the stadiums, which is important for any player.

GOWAR: Would you like to play in England if you had the chance?

MARADONA: Yes, for sure.

GOWAR: What do you remember of the victory over Scotland last year? It was probably your best match of the tour and the team's too.

MARADONA: Yes, the team was the most important part, playing brilliantly; we didn't give Scotland a chance to overrun us because all our counterattacks were half a goal, we hit the posts, we scored three goals that could easily have been five. The most important thing aside from all of us playing well was the team; we exchanged passes in all areas of the pitch and that led us to victory.

GOWAR: After the game, the English press all said you were the best young player to emerge since Pelé, which is not the same as comparing you with him. What do you say to that?

MARADONA: I don't think I'm Pelé's successor nor the best player in the world. I work to try and become a number one, but I don't take it for granted.

GOWAR: English fans were impressed by Argentina's victory in the (1978) World Cup and the behavior of the supporters. Do you think everything is forgotten about what happened in '66 (World Cup) with Antonio Rattín's sending off at Wembley and all that?

MARADONA: I can't give an opinion on that because I was six in '66, but Menotti, apart from correcting many defects Argentine football had on the pitch, also corrected it outside. Today an Argentine football delegation that's with Menotti doesn't think about spilling crumbs on the table, breaking a table or knocking over a chair or behaving badly on a playing field. That's already been talked about and analysed by Menotti and he tells us players, and all we have to do is rest at our base and go to the stadium as rested as we can be and play and play.

GOWAR: So the players are more thoughtful than before?

MARADONA: No, the players were also serious before but there was a different mentality; the coach might not say anything to the players and they might do as they pleased, no? Now the coach, when we go abroad, talks to us and is constantly telling us what we shouldn't do.

GOWAR: England's coach [Ron Greenwood] also favours attacking football like Menotti. Do you think this match with England won't have the traditional differences between South American and European football?

MARADONA: Yes, within South American football I think we are not as slow as it tends to be. Argentina now has dynamism, speed; you could say we're playing the European way, meaning that's the football César likes, but adding to it the skills we South Americans have.

GOWAR: In Argentina's game today there is no room for man-to-man marking. It's very unlikely that in the match against England they'll put a marker on you to follow you all over the field.

MARADONA: I think any coach dedicated to attacking can't do that. You see that the Argentina team never did man-to-man on anyone, even playing against Pelé. Menotti thinks that if we lose a man to mark another, he can't attack, he has to dedicate himself only to that player, so Menotti doesn't like that, so we're not going to do that with Keegan nor anyone; we'll play and if Keegan is unmarked we'll pick him up in zones, whoever is nearest, we're not all going to chase after Keegan!

GOWAR: This match is being played a month before the European Championship which is England's main objective. How do you think they will go into the game?

MARADONA: Today, anywhere in the world, teams want to beat Argentina because they are the world champions. We're well aware of that and so we prepare very, very well to face any team, England, or the best or worst teams in the world; there are no exceptions.

GOWAR: You're also going to play Ireland. You played against them last year when you came on for the second half.

MARADONA: We won 1–0 but really it was the game in which we created most goal chances on the tour.

GOWAR: Menotti started the match by fielding some reserves, right? But not in the team he put out against Holland or Italy?

MARADONA: Sure, it was because we were quite tired after the Holland game, which had been played at an infernal rhythm [a 0–0 draw after extra time that Argentina won on penalties]. We didn't get proper rest after that so he put out some of the other lads but they weren't reserves, we are all first-team players here. He made changes in the second half, [Américo] Gallego went on, I went on and I think we deserved to win, we hit the bar and missed a whole lot of goals. One time, I was alone facing the goalkeeper; I wanted to change the post [I was aiming at] and the ball went just out.

GOWAR: Now you're a superstar and wherever you go the center of attraction. Is the Maradona of today the same as the one six years ago?

MARADONA: Every time I'm asked that question, I say that the only thing that changed in Maradona is his wardrobe, because now I have clothes I didn't have before.

As a player you go gaining experience, learning more about your rivals, getting to know the pitch, the balls are

different, the one we might use in England from the one we
play with here; you go learning with each match, right?

GOWAR: What is your ambition now?

MARADONA: My ambition is to be champion with my club
here [AA Argentinos Juniors], then to beat England,* which
is our objective, that is to win all the matches on the tour and
then to think about the '82 World Cup with the warm-up
games we're having. But I don't like losing at anything and I
think the way the national team is working now we can win
everything because there is skill, and we are preparing to get
there in great shape.

---

* England won the game 3–1.

ON LEAVING NAPOLI

INTERVIEW BY BRUNO BERNARDI
LA STAMPA
SEPTEMBER 27, 1992
TRANSLATED BY ALLEGRA DONN

On July 5, 1984, Maradona was welcomed by tens of thousands of Napoli fans in the San Paolo Stadium. Maradona described the time he played there as his "resurrection," after a disappointing experience with Barcelona which he joined in 1982 from Boca Juniors.

According to the historian John Foot, despite the glory he found in Naples, much of the rest of Italy—especially the North, which was coming under the political influence of the Lega Nord—hated Maradona. And as Maradona's upstart Napoli side started to defeat the likes of Juventus, Inter, and AC Milan, he became a synonym for everything northerners seemed to despise in the poor South.

If there was a high noon for Maradona in Italy, it was the World Cup of 1990, which Italy hosted. Maradona was already souring on Italy, even Napoli. In the spring of 1989, he had requested that he be sold to Olympique Marseilles, which had been strongly courting him. Napoli's owner Corrado Ferlaino told Maradona: "If we win the UEFA Cup I promise I'll let you go to Marseille."

When Napoli won the UEFA Cup that year—their first-ever international trophy—Maradona expected Ferlaino to honor his word. Instead, Ferlaino told him to honor his contract to Napoli. When Maradona protested, Ferlaion—according to

Maradona—said, "No, no, no . . . I'm not selling you. [That promise I made] I just said to motivate you."

A war of words broke out between Ferlaino and Maradona and it was around that period—Maradona notes in his autobiography—that the first stories in the media linking him to drug addiction and the Camorra began to materialize. By the time of the 1990 World Cup—judging by the front pages of Italy's lively sports newspapers—Maradona was fast becoming the most hated man in Italy.

Italy drew Argentina in the semifinals. The game was played at the San Paolo Stadium. At a press conference on the eve of the game, Maradona said, "I don't like the fact that now everyone is asking the Neapolitans to be Italian and to support their national team. Naples has always been marginalized by the rest of Italy. It is a city that suffers the most unfair racism."

Maradona addressed Neapolitans: "For 364 days a year you are treated like dirt and then they ask you to support them."

The Italian media had a field day with this, stirring up further anti-Maradona rhetoric. The Napoli fans themselves were more diplomatic: MARADONA, NAPLES LOVES YOU BUT ITALY IS OUR HOMELAND, read one banner during the game.

The game, 1–1 at 90 minutes, went to extra time, then penalties. Argentina won 4–3 on penalties. One of the penalties was scored by Maradona. As John Foot observes in Kapadia's documentary, "That's the time when everything goes wrong for him in Italy. Italy turns on him. The protection he had collapses. The backlash is nasty."

In March 1991, after a game against Bari, Maradona failed a drug test. The Italian football authorities banned him for fifteen months. He fled to Buenos Aires, where the Argentinian law authorities subjected him to continual harassment and surveillance, including a short spell in jail.

Maradona called those fifteen months "among the most terrible of my whole life."

In July 1992, with the ban over, Maradona was determined to "detach [himself] from Napoli." Olympique Marseilles showed renewed interest in signing Maradona, as did Sevilla, which was now being managed by Carlos Bilardo, who managed Argentina in the 1986 and 1990 World Cups.

Maradona eventually extricated himself from Naples. He joined Sevilla. Just after his arrival in Sevilla, he spoke with Bruno Bernardi, a journalist for the Turin daily La Stampa, *who Maradona admired deeply.*

"Mr. Maradona, why did you betray us?" This firecracker of a question comes from an elegant Neapolitan lady, here in Seville for Expo '92. She is staying at the Hotel Andalusi Park, the luxurious Arab style residence on the road leading to Huelva, where Diego Armando Maradona and his entourage have established their headquarters. Also here is his new team Sevilla and Carlos Bilardo, the former Argentina coach, who strongly wanted him in Spain to be able to help the footballer and the man.

The lady can't believe she is facing the former king of Naples, insisting: "We all love you, why didn't you come back?" Maradona's eyes widen: "I didn't betray anybody: you all follow Ferlaino and not the players who bring you joy." Before surrendering, the lady begs: "Will you at least come and play a match at San Paolo?" The conciliatory Maradona says, "Yes, that's possible."

This dialogue acts as prologue to our interview lasting over an hour, that Maradona grants, prior to training and watching Sevilla play Logroñés, in the presence of his wife Claudia Villafañe, his manager Marcos Franchi, and Fernando Signorini, his physical trainer. We haven't seen him for over a year, since he "fled" Italy due to doping allegations, causing him to return to Argentina, where his use of cocaine acquainted him with the shame of arrest, bringing humiliation and pain upon himself and his family. Now, through football, he is searching for his own identity—the truest one. That spark of love for the ball is visible in him, painstakingly allowing him to beat the spiral of addiction. His toughest game has just begun: by playing, and with the affection of those close to him, he can win the battle once and for all.

BERNARDI: Who is Maradona today?

MARADONA: A man who made mistakes, who paid the price and found his balance again: I have experienced wonderful things, as well as problems that don't cancel out the good I have inside, allowing me to realize that I'm neither too big, nor as low as they would like for everyone to believe.

BERNARDI: A local paper reported that you allegedly owe half a million to Christine Sinagra: the backlog for the child support of Diego junior that the courts of Naples have recognized as your son.

MARADONA: [*Agitated, a wave of sadness crosses his face.*]

Marco Franchi is taking care of it. I am too happy with Claudia and my daughters Dalmita and Giannina to think about this poisonous tale.

BERNARDI: Diego has changed, but he hasn't changed about Ferlaino to whom he points the finger . . .

MARADONA: The club abandoned me at the most difficult moment of my life. I didn't even get a phone call from Ferlaino. I would have appreciated it, even with insults. Anything. Only in the last few months, after sending me messages through other people, Mrs. Ferlaino called my wife on her cell phone to try and resolve an issue that had become too bitter between us men. But Claudia remembered that the last Christmas we spent in Italy, she had called Mrs. Ferlaino crying—and against my wishes—to intercede with her husband who had denied us a vacation we had already booked in Madonna di Campiglio. But it was useless. The wheel turns: Ferlaino, afraid of the mistake he made, used his woman to try and make me change my mind.

BERNARDI: Would you have returned to Naples?

MARADONA: When I was desperate—against Claudia's, Franchi and the doctor's advice—I wanted to play again, even in Naples. I made the last attempt with the twenty-one conditions that concerned the man more than the money. I didn't even owe Ferlaino a dollar because with the new contract I had already played three seasons. Rather, it was Napoli that owed me $7 million, a figure that also includes the advance for 1992–93. A little goodwill would have been enough. When Careca, Crippa and De Napoli* telephoned me, they touched the depths of my heart. In Naples I have many friends, inside and outside of football. And it's only Ferlaino's fault if I'm at Sevilla.

BERNARDI: Ferlaino wished for you a future as an executive.

MARADONA: If I ever become one, I will not collaborate with Ferlaino. He and I are too different.

BERNARDI: Naples has given you so much but what did it take away from you?

MARADONA: Naples loved me in a suffocating way, without ever a moment of peace to let me breathe. I hoped, and they promised me, that after two or three years it would change, but instead the pressure increased. I don't blame the Neapolitans. I seized on the promise Ferlaino made me that if we won the UEFA Cup, he would release me a season early. He took it back. And that was when I freaked out.

BERNARDI: Juve would have done anything for you that season. Agnelli let it be understood, and Boniperti said you are the only great champion who hasn't worn the black and white jersey. You were almost on the verge of coming to Turin: What would have changed in Maradona's history if you had signed that contract?

---

* Diego's teammates at Napoli.

MARADONA: Juve was my great dream and I would have been the player who keeps talking and screaming on the pitch, dragging his teammates, the type of player missing since the days of Bettega and Tardelli, when Juve won everything. In Turin I would have collected titles, I would still be in a city where you can walk quietly down Via Roma, without being harassed, like when I was in Italy those first few months, yet in Naples I couldn't leave the hotel. Roberto Baggio is a champion, perhaps the only one along with Caniggia, who can become my heir, but he must suffer as he is currently doing for a couple of more years to gain experience and maturity. Juve is an extraordinary club and you have to take your hat off to the Avvocato.* He is too strong, miles away from Berlusconi.

BERNARDI: Now it is Milan that dominates and allows itself the luxury of sending Gullit to the stands.

MARADONA: Absurd. I have a lot of anger towards Berlusconi: he is an egoist who has six foreigners not so much for strengthening Milan, but to weaken the competition. He is killing football. I understand the power of what has hurt me so much, but Gullit doesn't deserve a similar treatment. And in addition to Ruud, the public is penalized by being deprived of seeing an ace like the Dutchman who brings them so much joy. If he is not needed, they should give him to Sevilla.

---

*   Gianni Agnelli, owner of Juventus.

BERNARDI: In Milan, Lentini's* market price dwarfs the one paid by Napoli to snatch you from Barcelona eight years ago. Is that right?

MARADONA: It is a consequence of the demands that Torino made. Lentini already seemed to belong to Juve, and Berlusconi took him away with a contract that could not be turned down. I gather Lentini earns even more than I do. He is certainly a great striker, but he's not a phenomenon.

BERNARDI: So is Milan unassailable?

MARADONA: It can repeat the Scudetto. Juve remains Milan's nemesis, however, it cannot afford to think of the future by acquiring perky young players; it must think about winning immediately and strengthening itself with players full of personality. To be clear, the club needs an Ancelotti type who dominates the pitch and puts psychological pressure on his teammates and on his opponents. The other teams are not ready to compete with Milan. Not Inter, which lacks a Matthäus from its best days to hope to win the UEFA Cup. Not Napoli: Ferlaino no longer wants to make it a winning team. Neither Sampdoria that lost Vialli. Not the Roma of my friend Caniggia. Not Toro that has a good squad, but doesn't need the scudetto.

BERNARDI: Do you miss our Serie A?

---

*   For a brief period, Gianluigi Lentini was the world's most expensive player, moving from Torino to AC Milan for 18.5 billion Italian lire.

MARADONA: Very much. But now I'm in Spain. I am thinking about Sevilla's game tomorrow against Matthäus's Bayern: you will see a great Maradona. I have also invited King Juan Carlos. And I'm thinking about my debut in the Liga, on October 7.

BERNARDI: Are you not aiming for USA '94?

MARADONA: It's early, and I have so many doubts. First, I have to regain my place in the national team for the World Cup which would be my last and which could be distorted by differences in climate and time zones. At Italia '90 we went to the final because Vicini didn't play Vierchowod: if he had been placed in defense, we would never have drawn. And I pray to God that Sacchi's Azzurri do not reach the heights of Milan, otherwise they will become the strongest and there will be nothing for anyone.

From fairy tale to a telenovela, it is a story that never ceases to amaze. Good luck, Diego.

MARADONA CONFESSES FOR THE FIRST TIME

INTERVIEW BY GABRIELA COCIFFI
GENTE
JANUARY 1996
TRANSLATED BY MARISSA COLON-MARGOLIES

Maradona described the following interview with Gente *magazine as one of the most important he ever gave. In it he talks candidly about his long struggle with drug addiction. It was an interview he said that he hoped his own children would one day read, in order to understand the struggle he had gone through.*

For interviewer Gabriela Cociffi—who was then deputy director of Gente—*it was not an easy interview to land. According to journalist Lalo Zanoni's account, she learned several months earlier that Maradona was going to be taking part in President Carlos Menem's anti-drugs campaign, Sol sin Droga (Sun without Drugs). She confronted Maradona and asked him whether he was going to talk about his own use of drugs. Wasn't he whitewashing the campaign if he didn't talk about his own problems? she asked. Maradona and Cociffi had a falling-out over this. But she was undaunted. Over the next few months, she approached people close to Maradona—including Gulliermo Coppola, his manager—who, while sympathetic, feared that a whole series of commercial contracts Maradona was involved in would be voided if he went public with his addiction. Maradona was still paying for Boca Juniors at the time. In the end—because Maradona respected her tenacity—he agreed to confide in her just before Christmas 1995. The interview was published soon after, in two parts. According to Zanoni, it was one of the "most shocking public confessions in the history of Argentine journalism."*

COCIFFI: How many times have you tried to get off drugs?

MARADONA: Many, many times. But it took me a long time to ask for help. And this didn't work in my favor. The main thing is to ask for help when you see that you're taking more and more. Because that's the thing, to be able to save yourself; there aren't that many options: you either don't start, or you start because you think you'll be fine, but you ask for help quickly. And this is the mistake I made. I kept believing I had it under control when I was killing myself.

COCIFFI: How long did you think you were fine?

MARADONA: Two years, two and half years, three years. And it was too much.

COCIFFI: Did you keep going without asking for help because you were a part of a group that did drugs?

MARADONA: No. Because no one forces another. He who wants [to take drugs], wants it. And he who doesn't want it, never ever accepts it. I wanted it, and this was my mistake. People tempted me to try it, but no one put a gun to my head and said "Take cocaine." And it's like that, like I told you; you know why? Because with cocaine . . . everyone hides their drugs so they can have them. You don't want to show others what you have, you don't want to share, they're "your" drugs, you understand?

COCIFFI: Why did you wait almost three years to ask for help?

MARADONA: Because I didn't know how to ask for help in time. I didn't know how. And today, I know that if I had brought myself to ask someone to help me get sober, it would have helped me a lot in my life. I would have been happier.

COCIFFI: You weren't happy?

MARADONA: Yes, I had many happy moments. But many were very painful. And do you know what I think today? That maybe I had to go through this pain, those terrible moments of suffering, to get to this present moment in which I can tell kids everything I went through. And I guess it was good for something, you know? My pain can help some kid who is suffering today. This is what it means to find light in the darkness. I want them to see Diego, not Maradona—he who took drugs, he who won everything, he who went to prison*—because that's "el Diego," the man who's sitting in front of you, and it's he who can tell people the truth and he who can help others.

COCIFFI: What's the difference between Maradona and "el Diego"?

MARADONA: Maradona can teach you how to take a free

---

* Soon after returning from Naples in 1991, Maradona was arrested for drug possession and jailed for twenty-four hours until he was released on bail.

kick. And Enzo Francescoli can also teach you to take a free kick and he doesn't use drugs. Or a lot of others can. But "el Diego" can also teach people this—the everyday struggle against drugs; Diego wants to fight side by side with kids looking for a way out. He's the one who can give them an assist, who can give them a hand.

COCIFFI: Who first gave you a hand?

MARADONA: Repression didn't help me at all, I already told you. It was awful. But then I began to realize that there was a way out. That there was medication, that there were relapses, but, of all things, I learned most importantly how to take refuge in Claudia, the girls above all—with the same fear that I told you about, the fear of them seeing me like that. I started to talk to my parents, I began to explain things because my father didn't even know what drugs were—"But what does it do to you when you take it?" he asked me. And look, some "intelligent informer" said that my father was to blame for all of this, and this person has zero idea of the things my father lived through, the things we all lived through . . . and I myself began to want to get sober more than anything. Because, in the end, when I stopped using for the night and wanted to sleep but couldn't, I said to myself, "Why did I start?"

COCIFFI: What made you most regret having started?

MARADONA: I asked myself—why did I begin to not want to see my daughters? Why did I begin to not want to go out with Claudia? I was afraid that Claudia would leave me. I was so scared. And that's where you begin to find a way out. I understand that you get clean with help, but if you don't want to stop taking drugs, you won't.

COCIFFI: It was your choice, first and foremost, then.

MARADONA: My choice, yes. Completely, and an absolute wish to stop using, to see yourself and say, "What am I doing? How is it possible that I can't stop using drugs? How can it be that I'm sinking deeper and deeper?" It was standing in front of a mirror after having taken drugs and saying to myself, "What am I doing here?"

COCIFFI: What happened on the day that the police went looking for you on calle Franklin?*

MARADONA: That day, when I was on Franklin, I was sleeping. It's a lie that the police found me getting high; it's a lie. I was sleeping so deeply that they had to pull me out of bed by the legs to wake me, because I hadn't realized they were breaking into the apartment. Look, what I'm telling you is that I was sleeping so deeply that when I woke up, I yelled, "Claudia!" because I had also taken sleeping pills, this I confess to you. But that day they invented a thousand of dark, untrue stories. I was in a bad state. It was a horrible comedown, but they said too many false things and it's not even worth recording them here, because none of these false stories will help kids who are struggling. The only thing I'll tell you

---

* Calle y Rojas, in the Caballito neighborhood of Buenos Aires.

here is that the reality of drugs is sufficiently dark and bleak, that for them to add things—I never understood why they invented so many stories.

COCIFFI: You told me that you never used drugs to play soccer. But when you were in Naples, an anti-doping drug test came back positive for cocaine. What happened there?

MARADONA: I went through some very twisted moments in Naples. When I tested positive for cocaine that time, it saved me. Maybe I did it on purpose unconsciously to free myself in that moment and be able to return to my country.

COCIFFI: Did you get high for that game?

MARADONA: No, I got high before the Napoli-Bari game.* But I knew I could be caught any minute. It was only a matter of time. I think I got high and hoped I'd test positive because it was the only way I could find to ask for help. And to return here [to Argentina].

COCIFFI: In Naples, you didn't have many options for getting out?

MARADONA: No, in Naples, I didn't have any way out. It got worse and worse. In Naples I had already won everything. Naples is a beautiful city, but it has a lot of problems, do you understand? In Naples, you have to be Maradona in order to

* Napoli played Bari on March 17, 1991.

live. If you are anything less than Maradona, they kill you. That's the way it is. Wherever I went, the mafia could be there, the camorra, but I was Maradona. I went in. I was their flag. They didn't love me because I was handsome or because I was good: they loved me because I beat the north of Italy. And because of this, "los capos" [the bosses] loved me because I made the people happy, the people they oppressed. But once a week, Sundays, I made the people happy. But in Naples, drugs were everywhere. They basically offered them to me on a silver platter.

COCIFFI: Statistics say that only 10 percent of addicts stay sober. Does that depress you? What does it make you feel?

MARADONA: It makes me feel that I have to fight against that 10 percent; we have to be many more. Many more of us are going to get clean. Because we can't tolerate drugs anymore. You get to a place where you say: "What am I doing with my life! I lose work, I lose family, I lose affection, I miss incredibly important moments with my family." And this is what I'm telling kids who miss school or miss their girlfriends' birthdays.

COCIFFI: What happy moments did you miss out on, Diego?

MARADONA: Many [*his eyes fill with tears*]. I missed out on changing Dalma's diapers. I missed many of my girls' birthdays because I was so high, I couldn't enjoy them. I lost nights with Claudia that I'll never get back because I locked myself in a room and didn't want to open the door. I lost all of those moments to cocaine.

COCIFFI: You only speak of cocaine. You never smoked marijuana?

MARADONA: I never smoked a joint; I never tried it. I didn't even know what a joint was: I went straight to the big time, you know?

COCIFFI: You didn't try heroin either?

MARADONA: No, thank God, no. Because I once saw some guys in front of our soccer practice who were about to inject heroin, and I couldn't do anything, because if you try to do something they can stick you with the needle. I saw them shoot up and how their eyes rolled back in their heads. It hit me hard, directly in the heart.

COCIFFI: And what did you think when you saw them lying there, being an addict yourself?

MARADONA: Look, both drugs kill. But heroin is awful: with it you can get killed easily. And I believe that if there's any difference, I want to mention it. Next to [fitness coach] Fernando Signorini's house in Italy, I saw a heroin addict hit his mother with a chair. Hit her hard, without mercy. "I'll go over there and stop him, I'll grab him and kill him," I said to Signorini. "Don't get involved, Diego, he'll pull a knife and stab you," Signorini answered. So I had to stand there, couldn't defend this lady who had her head bashed in. This guy had sold everything his mother had: the television, the radio, the decorations in the house. And because she didn't want to give him any more money to buy drugs, he grabbed her and beat her with a chair in front of us. It was terrifying.

COCIFFI: How much money did you spend on drugs? Did you ever do an accounting?

MARADONA: I never counted. But I spent a lot of money, a lot. I also made a lot of money. And I used drugs in accordance with how much I earned . . . A lot of kids sell everything they have in order to buy drugs, and dealers also give people drugs once, twice, three times for free, and once the kids are addicted, they want to sell.

COCIFFI: You said that you started by going straight to the "big time." The reality of being Maradona, the fact that the Pope chatted with you for hours and gave you a hug, the fact that Fidel Castro received you like a head of state, that people are dying to be at your side and that your hand is the "Hand of God": all of this didn't push you to start taking drugs? It didn't make you think, "I'll try it, I, who gets everything I want, I'll be able to manage this"?

MARADONA: No. I sincerely don't think so. Because I got all of those things because of soccer, no? And I knew that drugs were detrimental to my sport. I knew it, I know it and I will know it in the future. But it's true that, because I was doing so, so well, I didn't think at any moment that I would get into cocaine the way I did; if I'd known, I would have never done it. Because of this I want to say that you can't start. You can't get into drugs. I want to tell the kids that have already started to talk to their parents, or look for a friend, or go to the drug addiction prevention secretariat, or look for yourself in a magazine . . .

COCIFFI: Cocaine doesn't make you feel omnipotent?

MARADONA: It's a lie. It's a false image, a fake sensation of saying, "I'm on top of the world." You're left feeling completely empty. And I can prove it to people who think it's true, because I went through it and afterwards I felt like garbage. And I don't want kids to think that it's about flying high. I didn't feel the sensation of flying high. Only a moment of splendor that's false, false.

COCIFFI: After you made these statements, a lot of people applauded your courage and others criticized you, saying that you weren't the right "face" for the issue or the right person to speak to kids about these issues.

MARADONA: Look, Magic Johnson came out in the United States and said, "I have AIDS." And I say, "We're going to fight against the hell that is drugs." I don't remember having heard anyone criticize Johnson for this. And they hit me with this criticism. What happened before, when I hadn't yet said anything? Everyone criticized me, saying that I had done drugs, or that I was doing drugs and that I didn't admit to anything. And now, I come out and recognize it, and they criticize me again. You know what's going on? This is a two-faced country, hypocritical, and I'm the first to come out and speak openly about my illness or deepest suffering.

COCIFFI: Who was your first lifeline, the first hand you looked for to hold on to?

MARADONA: It was Marcos Franchi [Maradona's manager]. He told me that asking him for help, a lifeline, was a brave decision.

COCIFFI: Where did Franchi ask for help?

MARADONA: We began with the psychologists. It was here, in Argentina. But it turned out negatively for me. I felt tremendously oppressed because they isolated me from everything I loved. And I, who in this moment needed more than anything to be with the people who truly loved me. I think that they charged me a fortune because I am Maradona; they had me do things that didn't help me, didn't help me at all.

COCIFFI: You never thought of being hospitalized?

MARADONA: No, I didn't think of it. Because I was always convinced that, in order to get off drugs, I had to use my own willpower. I had to get clean by valuing myself more, which is something that I didn't do. I had to value myself. Because when you go into the hospital, afterwards, you can come out and want to conquer the world. In any case, I think a lot of people should go to rehab; that's where they can maybe find the willpower to get off of drugs that they can't find on their own.

COCIFFI: You had to love yourself more?

MARADONA: Yes, I think it's about that. Because I was trying to look for lost values. Values that you don't pay attention to anymore, that don't matter to you now, that you don't care about anymore. It happens because you're looking to recover beliefs or ways of living that you had at a very young age. To remember a lot of things. Not to be the same as before, but to remember how it was. To find the values that made you happy. Because at fifteen you want to change the world, at twenty-five a little less, at thirty you don't have the bandwidth to keep pushing forward like you could at fifteen. But also you know at fifteen years old that you thought about things in a clean way and at thirty you can't think that way because of drugs. I looked back, looked for my old values.

Because I believed, though I turned thirty and had this bad experience with drugs, that I had to put it together with everything I lived through at fifteen years old. It was like sitting in front of a screen and seeing the images of those two times together. The past and the present. Because time makes all of us change, but we shouldn't lose what we were, right? I think that my roots were also a part of my struggle to get clean.

COCIFFI: If you hadn't gotten out of Fiorito,* if you hadn't had all the fame and the glory, do you think drugs would have come into your life?

MARADONA: When we were young in Fiorito, joints didn't exist, much less cocaine, much less heroin. There was absolutely nothing. We were horribly hungry. We lived on such small scraps that if someone had offered us cocaine, we would have asked them for an alfajor [cookie]. It was very different. But, you know what? Today, there are drugs in Fiorito. I found out that a family friend sells drugs. I couldn't believe it!

COCIFFI: With everything you lived through, did you ever hit rock bottom?

MARADONA: Yeah, I hit rock bottom.

COCIFFI: From the rock bottom of drug addiction, what do you do to get clean?

MARADONA: Do you see this tile? I can't get to this tile and dig down deeper [*he touches the floor and scratches the tile.*] See? I can't go any lower. And I was there, against this tile. There was nowhere lower than where I fell, so because of this, logically, I had to go up.

COCIFFI: And what about all the people who stay stuck on the tile, the people who die or commit suicide because they

---

* Villa Fiorito, an economically deprived area just outside Buenos Aires.

also hit rock bottom? For example, Nirvana's Kurt Cobain, idol to a lot of guys, who ended up shooting himself in the head . . .

MARADONA: He did a lot of heroin. He was a lot crazier. Heroin isn't better or worse, but it makes you act like a monkey [*he shakes, imitating monkey-like movements*], the effort it takes to get clean, it's terrible.

COCIFFI: What made you feel that there had to be a way out?

MARADONA: My daughters' love . . . But to some people this will seem like a line. You have to cling to affection, you have to cling to love. Because you believe that you're a big shot when you're on drugs, and even though I was, because I'd won everything, I'd made it to the highest place a soccer player can, you can't be great if you aren't happy with those you live with, isn't that true? This is what I want to say to the kids.

COCIFFI: You seem sad, Diego.

MARADONA: Yes, it is really painful for me. Every time I think of this, I feel sick, I feel sick. Because I went through really hard moments, moments when I left Claudia alone, and this makes me sad, because I also wanted us to enjoy our time together with our daughters. And these are moments that you never get back. I can't go back! I lost Dalmita, I lost Giannina . . . There are things that won't come back no matter how much you want them to [*his eyes fill with tears once* *more.*] And now I don't want to lose anything else. I want to live well, I don't want to be on drugs during these moments, not now.

COCIFFI: You never thought that you might lose Claudia?

MARADONA: [*He takes a deep breath.*] I thought I would many times. I even thought that I had to leave Claudia's side for her to be happy. Listen to what I tell you [*his voice breaks*]. But she's the love of my life and I didn't let her leave or let her go.

COCIFFI: Did she ever tell you that she wanted to leave?

MARADONA: No, never. She never even threatened it to scare me. On the contrary. She was always at my side, even when I didn't want her there. But I thought at the time that she'd be happier far away from me.... It's the first time I say this, I've never told anyone. [*He smiles sadly.*] In reality, it's the first time that I say all of this. When, during the World Cup, she said: "I'd die without him," I say today that without her . . . I'd be dead. Without Claudia, drugs would have killed me. That's the big difference. Because out of love, Claudia says: "I'd die without him," but I would be dead today because of drugs. That's how it is.

COCIFFI: Tell me a story that reflects how Claudia tried to help you avoid using drugs.

MARADONA: Claudia never accepted it. You know what she did? In the Correa apartment, she locked the door and hid the key. So I couldn't go out. I was locked in. She didn't want me to go out. We argued. But she didn't let go of the key. So I took a sleeping pill and went to sleep, and that night, I didn't leave the house. It was amazing. Now, I sometimes watch her when she's sleeping. I'm Claudia's husband. And I feel proud that she's my wife.

COCIFFI: Taking pills was another way to search for an escape.

MARADONA: Of course, sleeping. What happened is that I was tired.

COCIFFI: Claudia never asked for help?

MARADONA: Yes, one day she went to a psychologist. But it was the first and last time she went. She didn't feel good or supported, nothing. There she got bad advice from Marcos Franchi, but he gave it out of love. He gave this advice because he's a good person, but it was a mistake.

COCIFFI: The other day you told me that the real reason you took drugs was because you felt acutely insecure. It's difficult to imagine Maradona insecure.

MARADONA: We're all insecure. Because we're all human. And the Maradona who was talking to you is the one everyone knows who got really far, the one who's famous all over the world. But the same things hurt me that hurt other people: pinches hurt me, the sun burns me, I get cold. And if I get caught up in drugs, I'm a victim or sick, like anyone else, although few people view me this way.

COCIFFI: Why is this your most important World Cup? Is this moment more important to you than other moments of glory in your career?

MARADONA: Because this is a World Cup of Life. I think the real World Cup is this one. The others, I already played. They're already forgotten or exist in people's memories. But they happened already. This is the World Cup that I want, for my team to be the boy who comes to me to say, "Diego, you threw me a lifeline," "Diego, you gave me an assist." I want someone to tell me this. Even if it's just one person, it's enough. I wish I could go house to house to speak with parents. I don't mind. I want to dive headfirst into this. This is why I thought of doing this with or without the president's support. I told him, "It doesn't matter if you give me your support, I want to do this anyway. I'm going to put a Sol sin Droga [anti-drug campaign] bumper sticker on the truck and go to Mar del Plata, to Cordoba, wherever."

COCIFFI: I've written down questions that some kids who are trying to get clean asked me.

MARADONA: What did they ask you? I want to know.

COCIFFI: One said, "Am I sick because I'm a drug addict?"

MARADONA: Yes, yes. You have to think that you're sick. You have to dramatize, exaggerate your situation. You have to feel sicker and sicker, and then, when you start to try to get sober, you feel better and better. The issue is that you think you aren't sick, and when you take drugs, you realize quickly that you're sick. When you're in treatment, you think you're going to quit drugs quickly. You've only just dipped your toe in the water and you think you're cured. Lie! This is the mistake. That's why you have to exaggerate. You have to value all the things you gain every day. You have to set a dream goal to achieve it.

COCIFFI: What goal did you set for yourself?

MARADONA: Return to soccer. And do you know what would be fantastic for the kids? To go back home. I was in my home. Maybe a lot of kids are hospitalized. Because of this, for them, the "Maradona's return to playing soccer" is go back home to their parents.

COCIFFI: What feeling do you have when you start to get your head out of the bottom of the well and start to see light?

MARADONA: Never believe it. You have to keep climbing the ladder because the light is up there. But drugs are much closer to you than the light. You can never forget this.

COCIFFI: Do you feel like a victim or did you seek out cocaine?

MARADONA: I think one is a victim of drugs. Because drugs are on every corner. And you are more of a victim than guilty. Because if politicians didn't let drugs pass through the airports, we wouldn't take them, or we wouldn't have taken them, or kids wouldn't take them. So don't believe you asked for it.

COCIFFI: Another question: How many relapses can an addict have when they're trying to get sober?

MARADONA: I say that you can stop. Relapse twenty times, but you get clean. And during those twenty times, you have to believe. I don't speak as "Papá" [in a patronizing way], because I'm the worst. I started trying to get clean three years after I started using. And do you know how many times I relapsed? If you fail one time, another, and another, it doesn't mean you're going to fail in the end. But you have to find capable people, people who can give you a hand. You have to decide to get clean. And you can't blame your parents. You can't tell them: "You don't understand my mambo, you're not my speed, you don't understand what I'm talking about." Because the person who has to want to get sober is the person infected with drugs, not his family.

COCIFFI: Did your parents suffer a lot when they found out?

MARADONA: Yes, they suffered a lot.

COCIFFI: Was it difficult for you to tell them?

MARADONA: Maybe less than I thought. Parents always surprise us.

COCIFFI: How did your family manage to not give up such a long fight?

MARADONA: They didn't give up because I always gave them hope. They saw that I tried and tried. And that's incredibly important. I don't want to say to the kids "get some balls," because I know how difficult it is. I, who've lived through the most awful things, I am telling you. You can't let yourself be won over by drugs. Letting drugs win is like jumping off the ninth floor, like killing yourself to avoid having responsibilities.

COCIFFI: In some ways, isn't taking drugs a slow form of suicide?

MARADONA: Also, also. But that's within your will. If you want to kill yourself, there are a lot of ways to do it. Taking drugs, of course, is one.

COCIFFI: Do you know that you've exposed yourself a great deal by talking about your experience with drugs publicly?

MARADONA: I know, but this is how I can reach the kids. I can't reach them if I act like a fake, hiding the drugs. Because I'll die before I act like a fake or a hypocrite. Because I want another Argentina for my daughters and for other people's children. I want an Argentina where people tell things as they are: where, if it's cloudy out, they don't tell us "it's sunny"; where, if there are no jobs, they say "we have problems"; where if a drug makes you sick, they tell us, "drugs are bad for you, they are bad," this drug is bad, it hurts people." That's the Argentina I want. And because of this I'm going to fight here in my space, which could be small or could maybe be big because I'm Maradona. You know what? For the first time I'm feeling like being Maradona can be more useful than just having forty photographers outside the door of my house. Now I want to be used by them.

COCIFFI: You know that if you miss even one game, or go out for a fun night with friends at a club, you're going to have thousands of eyes watching you and thousands of voices asking, "Is he out of control? Did he start doing drugs again?"

MARADONA: Even if I didn't do this, they were going to say the same thing. But now my commitment to the kids is a million times stronger than it was a month ago. Now we're in the fight together.

COCIFFI: Diego, do you want to use this to clean up your image?

MARADONA: I don't want to clean up my image, I don't want to be political, I don't want to be mayor of Devoto [an upscale district in Buenos Aires] or of Fiorito [the poor Buenos Aires district where Diego grew up], I don't want anything. I want to help kids find a lifeline.

COCIFFI: Do you want to be an example?

MARADONA: No, I'm not an example. Parents are an example. I'm not an example to anybody. I want to tell people about my experiences, the experiences I've told you about, so that these experiences can be useful. To give people an assist. I don't want to be anyone else's judge or father or anything. The only thing I want is to be an example for Dalma and Giannina. Nothing more.

COCIFFI: And what kind of example do you think you're giving them with these confessions?

MARADONA: The example of a father who can admit it when he's made a mistake. Who got into drugs and today regrets having done so. Of a father who felt so unhappy in the darkness of drugs that he began to look for the light, so that in his house there would be no dark corner. I want to leave them with the example of a father who loves them more than anything. And that he loved them so much that he fought and fought to get sober solely because he realized that drugs were keeping him away from them. I want to give them the example of a man who tried make sense of a story that hurt him a lot. And I think I found meaning [in it]: if only one kid quits drugs, if only one kid says, "Diego, you helped me," I'm done for the rest of my life.

COCIFFI: Give me a final message for the kids.

MARADONA: Don't start, because once you start taking drugs, it's very difficult to stop.

IN HAVANA: THE OTHER LIFE OF MARADONA

INTERVIEW BY DANIEL ARCUCCI
LA NACION
MARCH–APRIL 2000
TRANSLATED BY KEVIN BORTFELD

MARADONA: I think that drugs have to . . . We have to—we're talking about miracles, right? I think we must make them disappear. But drugs move a lot of money, and the world revolves around money, not feelings. The same people who say, "Look at Maradona, how he takes drugs!" are the ones who turn a blind eye as it passes through the airports.

ARCUCCI: Diego, is it also a miracle to make it disappear from your life from now on?

MARADONA: No. It's not a miracle that I'm off drugs. No. But it's hard, it's hard. It's hard, but you always have the hope of being able to live how I'm living right now.

ARCUCCI: Your current state, with your heart improved and being a little thinner, is good for you. But it doesn't seem like enough.

MARADONA: Look, this current state . . . To be clear, Dany, I'm talking about drugs because you asked me. But I know this will be of no use to anybody. Because from the article you write, everyone will just grab onto this part. They only want to know if Maradona is using drugs again in Cuba or not. Nobody is going to deal seriously with the problem. They don't want to know if the kid from the 'hood is sniffing glue, nor will they lower the drug addiction rates in Argentina. Those in Argentina who say they are fixing the problem are not. In Argentina, they propagandize with dolls, and dolls don't use drugs. They're all woven into it, and I'm a scapegoat, a smoke screen for those who let the drugs in and fill their pockets with money. It's a distraction, you know? Like Flaco Menotti said of football: it's about distraction. Rivellino looked to the right and passed to the left. They all went to one side and his teammate went alone through the other side. You understand?

The metaphor, yes, is understood. Especially when Diego Armando Maradona speaks with his regained voice, so different from the rasp that came from his throat not long ago, when his life choices had him hand in hand with death. He's speaking from Havana, but it can't be certain by the time this is read that he'll still be there. Hopefully. Everyone knows a day in the life of this man is equal to several for mere mortals. And he is still deciding how and where his story will continue, what will be the next chapter of his life's drama.

But for now, he's here, in the La Pradera International Health Complex, far from the boardwalk that overlooks the Caribbean but close to one of Fidel Castro's many Havana residences, in the middle of Siboney, next to Miramar. One can freely pass through the entrance, framed by two columns and lanterns above, next to the tall, pale, yellow wall intersecting the property, and take a right turn up to the hotel spa. But if you try to go farther to the left, things get complicated.

A pair of guards in green pants and white shirts, who rotate every other day, stop you and politely ask for identification. You need authorization to enter the buildings where patients undergo treatment, as well as the International Ozone Therapy Clinic.

In the background on the left are two houses occupied by Maradona and his entourage: House 1, where (Diego's well-known agent) Guillermo Cóppola and occasional visitors stay, and House 2, where Diego and Claudia live. Nothing fancy jumps out at you. The grass in the garden, dried and yellow, reflects the suffering of soil that hasn't had sufficient rain in three years. The houses, painted white, are simple and rustic yet comfortable.

Of course, for House 2 there are distinctions. In one of the side gardens, a massive black satellite dish points skyward. On the balcony, between two other small gray antennas, an Argentine flag flutters. Down below is a type of front patio with an improvised football-tennis pitch, lined off and baptized: Maradona had "La Bombonerita" written on the wall. Right next to the "stadium" is a little blue three-door Suzuki Vitara with tourist license plates parked under the relentless sun. Minor detail: It has no air conditioning.

Farther down, in front of House 1, sits parked an unmistakably official black Mercedes-Benz with a red plate of NH 0024. Like everything else—the houses, the treatment, the employees, the food—Fidel made it available to the group upon arrival to the island, with the faithful Alfredo at the wheel. He's accustomed to driving to the airport to pick up prime ministers and dignitaries and now does the same to collect precious goods arriving from Argentina: newspapers and magazines for the visitors eager for their hometown news, but also clothes and toys for the dozens of attentive Cubans who now have become part of the entourage.

Inside House 2, there's a special attention to comfort thanks to the goodwill of Canal 13, Telefe, and Torneos y Competencias: each broadcaster sent Maradona their respective decoders allowing him to watch Argentine television as if he was in Devoto "from the outside," he said. Three big screens are the focus of his living room: a professional monitor, a twenty-one-inch Samsung, and a gigantic thirty-eight-inch Sony, which was a gift from the producers of the program *Sorpresa y 1/2*. It's here, in front of his TVs, Diego spends much of his time.

Lounging on the flowery beige cushions of a two-seat wicker chair, remote control in hand, he becomes an eclectic program director: soccer, soccer, and more soccer, of any kind; newscasts, one after the other; NBA games, and if it's his beloved Tim Duncan and David Robinson and the San Antonio Spurs, even better; movies of all types; Discovery Channel, on any possible topic.

"I love Discovery. I love it," Diego says, pointing the remote at the television as if threatening it, eyes glued to a documentary about cinematic special effects. When the program ends, he finally lowers both the remote and his gaze and relaxes. He wraps himself in a salmon-colored blanket and drifts off to sleep. The humming air conditioner is an irreplaceable savior: outside at this siesta hour it feels like an oven on full blast.

Nearby next door, in one of the other three living rooms, sits Claudia Roxana Villafañe de Maradona, knitting. She hardly averts her gaze from the crochet needle, finishing the thirtieth square of a quilt of more than two hundred. She looks sideways when her husband's breathing gets a little louder and pays little attention to the TV, even less if there is a gossip show like *Telepasillo* on. It's still a while until *Calientes* comes on, featuring her daughter Dalma, which will demand all her attention.

But when Diego doesn't need someone watching over his sleep, she has time to dedicate herself to something she is passionate about. Seated in front of her Compaq Armada laptop, in the little room between the living room and the dining room, she communicates to the world: emails to find out how things are going with the official Maradona website under her direction; emails for the Brazilian Careca, for the Italian Ferrara, for the Colombian Higuita, for all the football greats on the planet who want to join in on the venture. And if it's not emails, it's the phone. Her latest model Palmtop would be the envy of any sports journalist.

But more than anything she chats with her daughters and their classmates. After hours in front of that computer, when Diego finally wakes, she shouts:

"Pa! Come here, it's Dalma!"

"Where, Ma, where?!"

"Here, on the computer!"

"Ah . . ."

Now it's night. A pleasant dinner is over, prepared by the personal chef, Rodolfo Chacón, and served amiably by the butler, Eduardo Carbonell. Both are quite young, and the Maradonas respond to their affability and good humor with genuine affection and trust. The table is always set with

enough settings for whomever is around and inevitably with
a fruit plate as a starter: orange, grapefruit, and mango. Next
to that, a big bowl of salad. Next arrives baked or roasted
potatoes.

"Do you know how Chacón prepares them?" Diego asks,
only to answer himself. "First, he boils them. Then he puts
them in a sock and smacks them against the counter. Later
he smacks them again after they come out of the oven. I hope
he doesn't use my socks . . ."

At the head of the table sits Guillermo Cóppola, cell
phone perpetually in hand, and to one side sit Diego and
Claudia, together. The dishes brought out might be skinless
chicken, rabbit, or even frog. For dessert, the old favorite
"vigilante" of fresh cheese and sweet potato jam. A lot of the
food comes from Argentina, even the condiments. It's impossible to get large yellow lemons in Cuba, nor diet products
or drinks. To drink there is pineapple juice, grapefruit juice,
or whatever juice Carbonell conjures up, preparing them in
an old, horrifically noisy blender in the middle of the dining
room, then asking each of them, "Does it taste good?"

After dinner, Carbonell brings another pitcher of pineapple juice to the living room, where Maradona has already
lit one of his Cohiba Robustos, at nine pesos each. Martalina
Pérez takes his blood pressure like she has all day long, checks
that he's taken his medication, and goes to the back room
where everyone—Eduardo, Rolfo, Alfredo, Maralina, and
the maids Clarita and Mirna—wait, ready for any request.

Diego whistles deeply, exhales the smoke without inhal-
ing, as he's been told, takes a sip of juice, and serenely listens
to the question.

ARCUCCI: Diego, are you afraid of death?

MARADONA: Yes. Yes, yes, I'm very afraid of death. I'm very afraid of death, but . . . since I almost died and didn't realize it, I now understand that out there, in death, you leave and that's it. There's no preparing for this, right?

ARCUCCI: You say that because you saw it up close . . .

MARADONA: I was practically dead. For one reason or another, I was practically dead.

ARCUCCI: And how would you describe your health today, if you had to rate it?

MARADONA: My health is good. I don't need it any better, either.

ARCUCCI: What! Why is that?

MARADONA: Yeah . . . I think that for the life I want, I don't need it to be better. I mean, I don't need to be 10 points out of 10 physically. I don't have to play. I perform well with my wife, ha ha! I don't think it's that important.

ARCUCCI: What don't you think is that important?

MARADONA: I don't think it's that important, um, to be in better condition. I mean, the whole world wants to be in better shape every day, but I cared more before because I played football. Now, I don't. I don't play anymore. Now I only need to stay in shape enough to play matches over there in Tortuguitas with the guys. That's my next goal.

ARCUCCI: And life? Are you afraid of it like you are of death?

MARADONA: No, no. I'm not afraid of life. When you have children, what you're afraid of is something happening to them. That's what worries me the most. That's why I'm selfish, why I say, "I'm dying? So what?" I would give anything so that nothing happens to my daughters, you know? But I think that's the logical attitude of a father.

ARCUCCI: Diego, even when you're sick, you say you're OK. What is the significance of that? Not knowing how to lose? Not accepting defeat?

MARADONA: I don't think because I say I'm fine but a person in front of me sees me as sick, that I'm a loser in life. You know what? Those who ask that question about me are the losers. They think that life is a game of winning and losing, winning and losing. And if you aren't like Maradona, you must destroy Maradona. If you're not like Che Guevara, you must spread lies about Che Guevara. And if your daughter doesn't end up like Sabatini, you're frustrated. It seems to me that we are mistaken. It's not about winning and losing. I think that it is life, and we must live it, everyone in their own way. Everyone with the same fears, the same worries, but without projecting those fears and worries onto someone else, someone else who is just fine. In terms of football, I don't play anymore, so I don't talk about winning or losing.

ARCUCCI: But, Diego, we aren't talking about football. We're talking about life.

MARADONA: Winning or losing in life? Who determines that? There's no *tabella* here, as the Italians say. No table of positions. No one decides. Nobody can say: "Miriam's father, who lives in Castelar, who did everything right, didn't go out at night, didn't smoke is winning." You know? It seems to me that it is not about winning or losing. On the contrary. There are moments. Like happiness, it's a moment. It comes, it leaves, it comes back. It shows up in the smile of your daughter, through a kiss from your wife, because Boca wins. It comes and goes. It's always changing.

ARCUCCI: From January up until now, have you begun to value things that you did not value before?

MARADONA: No, no, no. Well, knowing that you were dead and now you're still alive changes you, of course.

ARCUCCI: How did it change you?

MARADONA: In that . . . I had done things all wrong. It's not that I did them on purpose. Nobody wants to die. This is it: ask someone if they want to die, you'll see. Even someone in the electric chair is seized with fear. They've committed atrocities, crimes that get them sentenced to the electric chair. I mean, they are aware, they know what they did, and even they, who are sentenced to death, don't want to die, you know? Even they are afraid, even they cry for those last fifteen meters when they are taken to the chair.

ARCUCCI: What you went through in January, was that the most extreme moment of your life, where you felt closest to death?

MARADONA: Yes, yes. Because I had never been dead before. I had never been dead. But like I said, you're afraid of death but you don't realize it when it comes. And I don't believe in reincarnation or anything.

ARCUCCI: Did you ever think about committing suicide?

MARADONA: No, no, no! The one thing I'm not is a shithead. Drugs aside, I think that suicide is an escape; it would be to leave Dalma and Giannina, and that's why I'm content to be alive.

ARCUCCI: It never crossed your mind?

MARADONA: No, not at all. Not at all.

ARCUCCI: Not even when you were out of your mind on drugs?

MARADONA: No, no, no. I swear, for my daughters.

Sweat rings start to appear under his armpits, darkening his moss green Adidas shirt with red stripes that match a pair of Bermuda shorts of the same color. The TV is on but the volume low.

"Come on, keep going," he tells me, knowing there are questions left on the list, some from people who know of him but never have met or been with him, who have doubts about his behavior.

ARCUCCI: Don't you feel with what you did to yourself you let down a lot of people who look up to you?

MARADONA: No, no, no. No, the only ones I can disappoint are Dalma and Giannina. No one else.

ARCUCCI: Well, it's not a small thing. They, too, can be affected.

MARADONA: Look, since I have the unconditional love of my daughters, I don't feel like I've let anyone down. My old lady is still my old lady. My old man is still my old man. In any case, I gave football only part of what I had, and I could have given more. But I didn't want to. It was enough from me, right? They say, "Oh, look how great Pelé was!" or "Did you see? They left you off the list of the greats?" But I didn't play to be included in those lists. I played to entertain people in every match.

ARCUCCI: Well, sure, but you enjoyed being named the athlete of the century in Argentina.

MARADONA: How could I not! But I feel like it was the people who chose me. That's what I feel. Why did it cause such a fuss if not? Because it was more important for the people, for the majority, and not the advertisers, that I was given the award and not someone else, you know? For the people!

ARCUCCI: Diego, do you think that someday those same people will forget you?

MARADONA: Yes, yes.

ARCUCCI: How could that be?

MARADONA: I don't know if it's to forget, but to replace. Everything evolves, everything evolves. The kids today want the autographs of Romagnoli, of Riquelme, of Saviola. I don't know about mine. Well, it doesn't happen to me that much, but I see it happen with Beto Alonso, with Bochini. Bocha walks down the street today and nobody recognizes him. It bugs me. But, while it annoys me, I must accept that the kids live for one person to the next.

ARCUCCI: You inspire both hatred and love, but you always have admirers. Why do think, despite all that has happened, this devotion to you continues? Is it something you think about?

MARADONA: It's because . . . It's because I have always defended the people.

ARCUCCI: You think that's it?

MARADONA: Yes, yes, yes! I'm sure, I'm sure. I always defended the public. I've never been bought. I've been offered positions and never taken them. I never stuck my hand in the public's pocket. I tried to make them smile on the pitch. I fought with Grondona. I fought with Macri. The people who identify with me are thinking the same things that I say into the microphone. The voice of the people. Maybe I'm the voice of the footballing public. I don't want to take that any further. I'm going to keep speaking my mind about whatever I want. Yes, even if Moria [Casán] says I'm a loudmouth, because I pay my taxes and don't stick my hand in anyone's pocket.

ARCUCCI: Do you think there is something in your attitude, your way of being, that keeps others from saying no to you about anything or setting limits on you?

MARADONA: No. I don't think anyone should put limits on anybody. This is like one of those questions where a journalist interviewing someone whose relative has died asks, "How are you?" Seems totally out of line.

ARCUCCI: OK, that's your opinion. But imagine if someone who loves you very much, who wants the best for you, says to you: "Diego, don't do this. It's bad for you."

MARADONA: No, but . . . but I have my old man to say this to me. I'm proud of him. I don't believe anyone can tell me what to do. If this sounds like I'm full of myself, then I'm full of myself. But I don't believe that in our country anyone is in a place or has the courage or the balls to say such things to my face. We are a country . . . We are the way we are because we are the way we are.

"We are a country . . ." he says from Cuba, where a battalion of doctors continually hovers around him, even when he doesn't realize it or see them, every day. Every forty-eight hours Fidel Castro himself receives a written report on his health, of any progress or relapse.

From when he arrived nearly unrecognizable in a haze of sedatives to Havana on January 18 until two months later, the improvement of his cardiovascular problem has amazed the doctors. "Maradona arrived here with 28 percent heart functionality, and it has already reached 90 percent," they said in one rare moment they dared making a statement. Then his condition plateaued, "something logical and expected," according to the specialists. When he did not see spectacular improvements in the numbers or tests, Maradona's mood changed.

And so, on Monday, March 27, a coincidence occurred that could have changed the course of this story. The doctors, deciding this stage of the treatment was finished and other conditions needed to be met for the next, wanted Maradona to return to Buenos Aires. Maradona, having felt he was being pressured too much, had already decided to return to Argentina. On Tuesday, March 28, there was a meeting in the living room of House 2 between Dr. Pedro Llerena, the clinic director, and Maradona. It lasted very little time.

MARADONA: I wanted to leave here, yes, because the doctor talked to me in a way I didn't like. So, since I'm a hothead, I jumped up and said: "Thank you very much for everything. I won't be bothering you anymore. I'm going back to Buenos Aires." And that's where he appears, Guillermo, Guillermo Cóppola, the devil, the evil one, to calm the waters and make us understand what's best. This is the kind of help I am talking about, the kind that matters.

ARCUCCI: Do you feel they have helped you enough? Or, with this attitude of yours, are you not even interested?

MARADONA: Nobody's helping anybody.

ARCUCCI: But Diego, you asked them for help.

MARADONA: I know who to ask for help.

ARCUCCI: Who do you ask?

MARADONA: I ask Guillermo for help, and my relatives, because I know they love me. I can't ask for help from someone who says he'll help me and then goes talking to the newspapers because I'm Maradona. The great geniuses who say they will help you, why aren't they helping the kids in the 'hood sniffing glue? It's because helping Maradona is easy. Maradona is going to pay them, you know?

So, yes, I've looked for help more than once and haven't found it. I haven't gotten it. I went to Europe to see Professor Banks, Van, or something like that [he is referring to Dr. Harutyan Arto Van], who was the best around. We spent $60,000 with Guillermo on flights, accommodations, everything, because I had made a promise to Dalmita.

Two days later, when I woke up in the morning and turned on the television, I see Professor Van, the famous Professor Van, giving a press conference. I confronted him and said: "How is it, genius, that you haven't even drawn my blood but you're already blabbing everything to the press?" And you know what he said? "I'm sorry, I couldn't stand the pressure from the media. They all wanted to know." Son of a bitch! He was overwhelmed in forty-eight hours by the same pressure I've endured for twenty years. "It turns out I'm more of a professor than you," I said.

The man had declared into microphones from around the world: "Although Diego fell into the trap of drugs, his core problem is existential. If he were a typical junkie, in ten days he wouldn't be able to do a thing. My job is to strengthen psychological immunity for ten days so that he can withstand existential crises. In this context, the issue of drug addiction fades to the background. He told me he never suffered from withdrawal. It may seem odd that he traveled to find a cure, but what Maradona wants is to become a model father. His problem is the desire to take drugs. In other words, he's too weak to resist that urge. Our job is to make him strong.

Maradona has a deep desire to break the vicious cycle that has led him to drugs. He turns to cocaine when he feels overly pressured, not because of a physical addiction. He feels vulnerable. He is psychologically weak but determined to move ahead and he will succeed. Despite having won everything, he is not a happy man. He considers himself a loser. He has a hypersensitive personality. He comes from an extremely honest and loyal background."

ARCUCCI: Well, Diego, you can't complain now. If there's anyone different from what you've just described, it's these people. Here, the clinic director gets eighteen dollars per month salary, and you don't even have to pay it. Plus, they are incredibly discreet.

MARADONA: Of course, of course. That's why when I speak of the dignity of Cuba, it's because I see it, because I know it, because I feel it. Because I have lived it every time I've come here. Hey, I came here when I was on top of the world, the world champion, and also now when I'm in bad shape. That's why the Cubans are with me. Because while it's true that today Cuba is more in the spotlight, the international press is looking at Cuba, they love me because I came here when nobody gave a damn about them.

ARCUCCI: That's fine. But we are talking about recuperation, about healing. Do you think they can help you further? Are you going to let them do it?

MARADONA: Yes, yes. For sure. But I can't just stop being myself when a doctor comes to talk with me. I am in a read-justment process. Re-ad-just-ment. Who has the right to tell me I can't go dancing, huh? I go out with my wife. But just because I go out, nobody needs to say, "Look, what he's up to." I'm tired of this story people want to assume, that "he's messed up again" and stuff like that. And they include my wife in it, too, right? I promise you, if anyone who says that Claudia takes anything, I'll punch them in the mouth.

ARCUCCI: Well, people also wonder how Claudia puts up with Diego going out, with Diego this, with Diego that. Why does she put up with it?

MARADONA: Because everyone goes out. Everyone goes out, but nobody takes their picture. Maybe I go out with her approval. That's how my life is. I chose her and she chose me. And I would kill for Claudia. Kill. That she said once, in one of my worst moments, "Without him I die," for me means eternal love. Maradona without Claudia is not Maradona.

ARCUCCI: Nobody has the right to tell you, if they see you dancing in the Habana Bar, for example, "Diego, this is bad for you"?

MARADONA: I think that we talk about others and don't pay attention to ourselves. And this is very Argentine, you know? Very Argentine. In other words, we are who we are. We hide, we put on the face of the do-gooders and then elect Aldo Rico minister of security or mayor. I think there's a big contradiction in our country. But they say that of me. Me, OK, because I have my craziness. But a country shouldn't be crazy or conflicted. Let Maradona, who is crazy, be conflicted.

ARCUCCI: Diego, what's your goal in being here?

MARADONA: My goal is the tranquility of Cuba, to not get mixed up in the constant press conference that is Argentina.

What the Cuban doctors say in 2000 sounds more cautious but just as accurate as what the Armenian doctor Diego spoke about revealed. Psychiatrist Ricardo Gonzalez Menendez forces us to read between the lines: "There are many reasons why he can be rehabilitated. Because of his willpower, because of the great love he has for his family, because of his great love of sports, because of the strong feeling he has that he can be a positive example in the future. For everyone, a sense of home is important, and his is very well-developed. This is an emotional support network. Despite what the international press says, there is much to make us think that when Diego decides to follow a treatment properly, with the necessary amount of time it takes, and finally decides to not take drugs anymore, he will succeed. I think that right now, he is appreciating his cardiovascular improvement. The danger in this is to think that he's already overcome his problem."

ARCUCCI: Diego, you always say that you were not, you are not, and will not be an example. Never. But what happened to you in Punta del Este ended up being an example of what drugs can do to a human being.

MARADONA: It could be. It could be that it's an example, but I don't think it was worth anything. But let's be clear that what happened in Punta del Este was not only a drug problem. It was a mess, I made, self-medicating. It was dangerous, and even more so because of the drugs I already had in my system. It really knocked me out.

ARCUCCI: Well, that's obviously what I meant.

MARADONA: But I've said this already many times. Do you know why you can't talk about drugs in Argentina? Because every time I say something, the doctors who supposedly cure drug addiction charge more. And kids keep dying. And more and more drugs are taken, more and more are sold. More and more pass through airports and they turn a blind eye, you know?

ARCUCCI: When you are high are you self-aware?

MARADONA: Yes, yes. Of course, I'm aware. That's why I don't go out when I'm like that. Anyone who says they saw me high is lying. Not even in Punta del Este, not even when I was at my worst.

ARCUCCI: And now, here, how are you doing?

MARADONA: Good, good. Bored because this takes time. I want to live my own life. I don't want a doctor or anyone to dictate it to me. And I want to enjoy my daughters, you know? That's all there is to say. But I don't want it to be dictated to me, Dany. My whole life I did it my way, as the song says. And I'm going to die my way.

ARCUCCI: Sooner or later.

MARADONA: No, no, later. Later. What I don't want is to be a burden on my daughters or end up, as I always tell Giannina, in a nursing home.

ARCUCCI: No one would bet on you ending up that way.

MARADONA: No. Never, never, never.

ARCUCCI: What things did you learn and what things did you lose because of drugs?

MARADONA: I lost a lot of time spent with my daughters. But it can be made up. Maybe, being who I am, I lost the chance to give the fans a few more nutmegs, a few more sombreros. But I don't regret it because I made my life how I wanted. I don't want it to be dictated to me, you know? Maybe if I hadn't made so many mistakes, I would have been the greatest . . . ha, ha, ha.

ARCUCCI: Are you waiting for me to say, "But you are the greatest"?

MARADONA: No, no. Seriously, if I had taken better care of myself, I would have been the greatest. But I've learned, I've learned. And notice that of all the friends I've had, of which there weren't many real friends, none can say I bullshitted them. I have always been the same, out in the open like a streetlight, because being Maradona, I can't hide. You can't be a bullshitter being Maradona.

Dozens of cards arrive per day to that name. Claudia opens them one by one and answers them with an autographed photo of Diego. There's also a red and white ball signed by the greatest Peruvian football players in history wishing him luck. And a gigantic hand carved in wood, a gift from Cóppola's in-laws. It's of his hand, the "Hand of God," the one that scored the goal against the English.

ARCUCCI: Was there any point in your life, in these forty years, that you felt like you didn't want to be Maradona, to call yourself Maradona?

MARADONA: No, no, no. First, because that's my old man's name. And I've always taken pride in representing Argentina abroad. But not even in the bad times, in the worst moments, did I feel the name Maradona was too heavy.

ARCUCCI: Not even when you were in prison.

MARADONA: No, not even when I was arrested. The first two who came to see me then were Claudia and my old lady. And they threw themselves on me. Once as a joke, Claudia said she was taking my house key and not letting me in anymore. And my mom, who was there, said: "Hey, the baby's room is ready, right?" I mean, I'm saying I'm not that bad. I also see it in my sisters' eyes, the way they look at me, how they love me. Ana is fifty years old, and we kiss each other on the mouth. We need each other. I talk to them and ask how Ana is, how Kity is, how Mary is, how Caly is. I was able to buy a big house because God gave me that chance, because he said: "Everyone can be here." We always remember a place like this, much smaller.

With his arms, he seems to be describing only the living room in which we are seated, no more than three square meters.

MARADONA: Yes, smaller. Eight of us slept in a room like this. Eight of us slept and no one got in the way. No one. That's why when they talk . . . I don't judge. I don't judge people.

ARCUCCI: And how do you judge yourself?

MARADONA: Huh? How do I judge myself? Like a man from the 'hood who relied on himself the best he could and spit the rest out like anyone in my position would, nothing more. But one thing is clear: don't treat me like a fool, understand? Because to me, my old man, who didn't finish primary or secondary school, is the best man in the world. He is the purest man in the world, and I wish there were many men in the world like my old man. And yet these educated geniuses, their professors, everyone, make a living fucking over the public.

ARCUCCI: And Cóppola, judged by everyone, how do you judge him?

MARADONA: Easy. No more agent and client. From now on, starting now, we are partners, in everything. He is my unconditional friend. He is my brother. He is my old man. I know everyone blames him for what happened to me, but let's be clear: I never did anything because of him. No one put a gun to anyone's head. My friend is the last one to incite me to do anything I don't want to do. We're here as friends enjoying good things, not ugly ones, you know? This is what I want people to understand, those that want to understand. It's simple: When I do something stupid, don't blame Cóppola. Don't blame Cóppola. Because aside from making Guillermo look like Lucifer, they underestimate me, as if I don't know how to make my own decisions at forty years old. They think Guillermo brings me drugs, that Guillermo—and he is the one always taking care of me! What he does is help me, not pressure me.

There is always a surrogate family around the Maradonas. This time it's the Tedeschis, Argentines who have lived in Havana for nine years. Alfredo, a cameraman for Reuters, began his relationship with Maradona in the worst way. A punch broke his car window outside a mall where they were trying to take photos of Diego shopping. After apologies were made, a relationship was born that made the Tedeschi house the go-to place for a nostalgic asado or tango karaoke, or a boat trip to breathe in the unique Caribbean air. There's always, always someone to come help when the building is falling apart.

ARCUCCI: Who did you go to in your most difficult moments?

MARADONA: I think of God, of my God, of the only God.

ARCUCCI: And how do you imagine your God?

MARADONA: No . . . Sometimes I talk to him, you know? But I don't ask him for things. I talk, and I tell him the things that happen to me. And sometimes I lock myself in the bathroom and, and . . . I talk. Or sometimes I mention it to Claudia. But no, I don't ask for anything. He has given me too much to ask for anything and, and . . .

ARCUCCI: Your biggest daily frustration is not being able to play football?

MARADONA: Yes, but not professionally. This thing that Maradona is being like this because he doesn't play anymore isn't true. For me, the only thing that hasn't disappeared is my passion for football. It used to happen in Fiorito: when I saw a ball, my eyes lit up. It still happens today. And anywhere: at the Boca stadium, at River's, at my country house in Moreno, in Tortuguitas. I've never gotten tired of the ball, and I never will.

ARCUCCI: By the way, when you were a kid, how did you imagine yourself at forty? Still a footballer?

MARADONA: No. I thought I was never going to make it, heh. No, a forty-year-old man cannot play football anymore at the level I played. I like to remember things, yes, but not plays. I prefer the anecdotes of my teammates, everything I experienced around football. That's perhaps why there isn't a single player who has a bad thing to say about me. Because

I have always treated them with respect like they have to me. In other words, to me, they were all Maradonas, you know? If I made ten [pesos], everyone else on the team had to make five. And that was ten times more than they ever expected. They always appreciated me for that. I think that God has given me more than enough by making me a footballer, and I'm very proud to have been one.

ARCUCCI: And at sixty, how do you see yourself?

MARADONA: An old kid, heh, heh. If I reach sixty, I'll throw a party for fifty thousand people, heh, heh. But no, I imagine myself watching videos with my grandchildren. And like my old man, for sure.

Claudia, barely looking up from her knitting, says, so that it can be heard:
   —You're the same, Pa . . .
   —Heh. I'm not talking about physique, Ma . . .
   Diego feels like he has talked too much, his heart on his sleeve. He listens to the final question, the usual one, a footnote, a goodbye.

ARCUCCI: What are you missing?

MARADONA: What am I missing? Moving ahead. To continue improving with what I'm doing, continuing my readjustment, improving my heart. And I'm missing . . . I'm missing working in football, which is what I want.

A REUNION WITH GARY LINEKER

INTERVIEW BY GARY LINEKER
BBC TV
MAY 2006

In 2006, it was as if Maradona was a new man. After stomach stapling surgery and rehab, Maradona lost a lot of weight and swore that he had overcome his drug addiction. During this period, Gary Lineker, one of England's greatest center forwards who played on the England side that lost to Argentina 2–1 in the 1986 World Cup quarterfinals—the game during which Maradona scored his infamous "Hand of God" goal—ventured to Buenos Aires to track down Maradona and talk about that game. Lineker, now a popular broadcaster for the BBC, had tried, years earlier, to meet Maradona in Argentina, but the interview fell through. In March 2006, Lineker finally managed to get his audience with Maradona, when they had the opportunity to discuss the two goals Maradona scored against England.

LINEKER: '86, probably the highlight of your career. You got through to the quarterfinals where you played us, England. There was a lot of buildup for that game because, of course, the Falklands/Malvinas beforehand. Both sides said at the time that wasn't important. Was that true for you?

MARADONA: It seems to me that everyone surrounding us was talking about the Falklands/Malvinas. We just wanted to play a football game. I'm not going to resolve anything thinking about something else other than winning. Winning the game against England.

LINEKER: It was your hand? Or the hand of God?

MARADONA: It was my hand. With this I don't mean any disrespect to English fans, but this is something that happens. We used to do this. I had scored goals before in Argentina with my hand; it was a goal that I couldn't reach it and Shilton was already there, so I couldn't head it, so I did like that [*repeats motion of scoring with hand*]. And I moved my head back and I started running because I started to run at first and Shilton didn't realize and the one who told him is the sweeper, he was the one who sees my hand. When I see the linesman running, I go out shouting, "Goal!" and I look behind me to see whether the referee took the bait and he had, so that was it. "Come on, come on it was a goal!"

LINEKER: As you ran way and you were looking around at your teammates, do you think they knew?

MARADONA: My teammates did notice and they didn't come over to celebrate with me. I was saying: "Come on, come on! Hug me. Let's do it properly. Let's go the whole way!" Hoping the goal would be allowed. Thank God it was.

LINEKER: In England that would be regarded as cheating; they would say you know that's totally against fair play. How do you see that?

MARADONA: No, I don't think it's cheating. It's cunning, cheekiness, it can be handling the ball or . . . it's not cheating. I believe it's a craftiness. Maybe we have a lot more of it in South America than in Europe. It's not cheating.

LINEKER: Why did you say, "the Hand of God"?

MARADONA: Because God gives us the hand, because he gave us a hand. Because it is very difficult not for it to be seen by two people, the referee and the linesman, so that's why I said it was the "Hand of God."

LINEKER: Personally, I blame the referee and the linesman not you, if that counts . . . The second goal is probably the one and only time in my whole career that I felt like applauding the opposition scoring a goal. Your best goal. [*Maradona shakes Lineker's hand in gratitude.*]

MARADONA: It's the dream goal. As footballers we always dream of scoring the best goal in history; we dream it and we have it in our heads. And the truth is to score that goal for me was fantastic and in a World Cup. Incredible.

LINEKER: And even better as it was against England?

MARADONA: When you talk about playing against Italy for example, Uruguay or Brazil, it is much more complicated to do the move that I did while playing against England. Because the English player is a lot more noble, much more honest on the pitch.

LINEKER: Just one thing. I think they were trying to kick you, they just couldn't catch you.

MARADONA: Of course, was it Peter Reid? That's right, he wanted, you can see him, you could just see him trying but he's just not making it, he couldn't reach. And then when I faced the sweeper, what was his name, Fenwick, the one with the long hair, when I faced him I saw that Valdano and Burruchaga passed me from over there, so I dummied him; I dummied him and Fenwick didn't know what to do, whether to go this way or that, and when I kicked it forward I saw Shilton coming out and I dummied him, like this, and Shilton spread out like this; I just touched it like this and Butcher was closing in. He gave me a kick on my right leg but when butcher came closing in, I'd already touched the ball.

LINEKER: You went on to win the World Cup, highlight of your career?

MARADONA: It was. I think it was the moment of glory. Of total glory. World Cup in which we weren't the favorite but we became stronger as we progressed through the tournament, game after game. Personally it was the ultimate achievement. The ultimate.

LINEKER: A lot of people around the world say that Maradona won this World Cup on his own. That they didn't have a good team, what do you say about that?

MARADONA: No, no, no, we had a great team. A good team became a much greater one because of my presence. I recognize that. But I'm also totally convinced that I didn't win the World Cup alone, that's a fact. Without the team's contribution I might have won the game against England, but not all the games we won after that.

THE TRUTH
BY DIEGO

INTERVIEW BY GIANNI MINA
JUNE 2013
TRANSLATED BY ALLEGRA DONN

Journalist and documentary filmmaker Gianni Mina, a man whose left-wing politics and great sympathy and passion for the struggles of the peoples of Latin America synchronized with Maradona's own political sympathies, built up an incredible bond of trust with Mina during his years in Italy. Maradona gave some of his most candid interviews in Italy with him, many while Mina was working for the Italian state TV network, RAI.

The following interview was conducted in 2013, while Maradona was living and working in Dubai. In this interview he reflects on his experience coaching in the United Arab Emirates, his stormy time managing the Argentinian national team at the World Cup 2010, and his opinions on the greatest players of the present day, namely Lionel Messi and Cristiano Ronaldo.

MARADONA: Today I am a normal man, I can walk quietly down the street, I can go to the supermarket, I can talk about football and about everything that I want to do in my life. When I was playing football . . . there was always someone who challenged me, but I reacted every time: I had no difficulty in rebelling against what I saw and did not like in my life.... But now I live in Dubai, in the Arab Emirates, Gianni, far away from my country, after having had a wonderful experience as a manager of the Argentinian national team.

In my country, however, the national sport is not football, it is envy, hatred . . . and this led me to this place, Dubai, where instead I found peace, respect and even affection. A place where they know how to value you for what you've done and for what you do, because even if they judge you according to the legend you have created around yourself, the fact remains that if you don't work today, you don't get paid. From afar, we think: "The Arabs will accept anything," but in reality, this is not so. Arabs eat better than we do!

There is bitterness in the voice of the Diego Maradona I find myself in front of today. In Dubai he is fine, he seems in good shape to me, even peaceful, but there is a hint of melancholy and disappointment in his eyes. It's as though he has struggled to absorb the controversies over his role as the head coach of the Argentinian national team, culminating in their elimination from the 2010 World Cup quarterfinals, which they lost to Germany. He tells me that he still loves football very much: the problem, if anything, is that he has it with the men who run it.

MARADONA: I still don't like them, and I told [Michel] Platini so once. Why are they choosing two venues at once for two consecutive world championships, Brazil and Russia? Why are the top executives old? Are they afraid they're going to die in the period between two world championships? Before they would choose one venue at a time, now two. Perhaps they're afraid they won't collect the money meant for them?

There is a lot of match-fixing that nobody dares to talk

about. Everyone pretends to be stupid. Gianni, there are 180 fixed matches every year in the world. It's a huge problem that FIFA and UEFA have. Meanwhile, Bayern Munich, Real Madrid, Barcelona, become champions, and it goes on like this, but it's the people who pay. I don't want to see a fixed match, I want to see a real match: a match with surprises and spectacular goals.

His outspoken views about FIFA are well known, as is the lack of love the top executives have for him, from Havelange to Blatter. And Diego is a man who doesn't forget.

MARADONA: Havelange was a water polo player. And he ran us footballers. He never kicked a ball in his life. Blatter, each time he invites me, he invites "the family." But to me "the family" smells a lot like the mafia, you know? It's like finding Robert De Niro or Al Pacino in a film praising the mafia, the FIFA mafia. Instead, I think that, in football, dribbling is only needed on the pitch: prowess is to pretend you're going right and instead you dive to the left. This is the only deception acceptable to fans. There are other deceptions which, on the other hand, cannot be tolerated, like letting one team play at noon and the other team at nine o'clock at night . . .

I know what he is thinking about: at the 1990 World Cup Italy, when Argentina played regularly at four in the afternoon, while the Azzurri always took to the field in the evening, when temperatures were much more acceptable.

MARADONA: And despite this unfairness, I want to remind all Italians that we were the ones who wiped out Italy. I'm not saying this to be provocative . . . The point is that the final had to be Italy-Germany. It was sold to the world as the "grand finale." And we were in very bad shape, Gianni. I had a tear, Ruggeri, a groin injury. Caniggia was unable to play the final because he had broken the hand ball rule and had therefore been disqualified for one round . . . But Italia '90 is nothing compared to what is happening today . . . Look at the Confederations Cup,* for example: you can't pit Tahiti against Brazil or Spain, burying a poor goalkeeper with goals. We try to propose more credible matches, so that people put more trust in the soccer players. People like Blatter, Havelange, Grondona . . . should have retired a while ago and not be in charge of an important structure like FIFA.

I point out to him that because of his accusations against FIFA, he ruined part of his career, but Diego, despite being perfectly aware of this, would do it again in exactly the same way.

MARADONA: And do you want to know why? Because, Gianni, I sleep peacefully. I can afford it because when I went out on the pitch I gave it my all without hurting anyone. It's the others who do not sleep: they are always awake, to do harm to football.

---

* Considered a dress-rehearsal for the World Cup a year later, these tournaments would involve the host country of the World Cup, the winner of the previous World Cup, as well as the winners of the regional championships. FIFA scrapped it in 2017.

Hearing him speak with so much passion and anger, even years after his retirement, I suddenly ask him if champions still exist in football. Does it bother him a little to always only hear about top players.

MARADONA: Yes, I say that the great player still exists, but he is no longer involved and tied to those who feed him, i.e., the people. There is a big difference between when I was playing and the present. Today the footballer believes he must play football and that's it. But no. For me it's correct that he supports his true source of income—the people, and that he protects those who will come after him. It's not because you're the best that you must always say yes to FIFA, UEFA, the federation of your country, or to an executive who has never kicked a ball. Instead, Gianni . . . I believe that the great player is still there today, but that he doesn't go beyond the ball, beyond training. In short, he does not expose himself.

Let's talk about Pelé. Of the controversies and demonstrations held in Brazil in the lead up to the Confederations Cup,* the World Cup, the Olympics. Again, Diego does not keep quiet.

---

* In the run-up to the Confederations Cup in Brazil 2013, massive protests broke out in Brazil, targeted at FIFA and the Brazilian government for investing huge amounts of money into the World Cup and Olympics to the detriment of spending targeted at public services, such as housing and health care. Eduardo Galeano—a writer Maradona admired deeply—said, "Brazilians, who are the most soccer-mad of all, have decided not to allow their sport to be used anymore as an excuse for humiliating the many and enriching the few. The fiesta of soccer, a feast for the legs that play and the eyes that watch, is much more than a big business run by overlords from Switzerland. The most popular sport in the world wants to serve the people who embrace it. That is a fire police violence will never put out."

MARADONA: Pelé is not loved by his colleagues, and this is very serious. He has always been on the side of the great "potentates," such as FIFA and UEFA and has never been with people. When he was asked for money for Garrincha, he just let him down. This was told to me by his wife Elsa Soares, the singer. One day she approached me and told the story. They went to Pelé and asked for help, but he did not answer their call. Certainly everyone does what they want with their life, but Pelé was at the top and he could have done something about it. To tell the truth, Pelé was prisoner of his own time: Romario already said it, Ronaldo said it, Ronaldinho said it. That's the reason why Pelé is not loved in Rio, because everyone knows the Garrincha story. He thinks he has the support of the people, but when he has to prove it, he's in favor of FIFA, as he did in the case of this Confederations Cup.

Knowing that Diego is a friend of the former president of Brazil Lula, and a supporter of the social policy that Brazil, along with other Latin American nations, is trying to push forward, I ask what he didn't particularly like in the management and organization of the Confederation, and the World Cup.

MARADONA: Well, I believe that Brazil deserves the World Cup, as well as the Olympics. It's all very nice, Gianni, but to embark on projects like this you need to have the approval of the people and it must be strong enough so that everyone can enjoy these major sporting events. Otherwise, what's the use of entertaining people with these events, if the people have nothing to eat? I say this because I come from Argentina, where there are super rich politicians and very poor people. It's as if you feed those who are hungry today and then you confuse them for a whole week, entertaining them with football, horses, casinos . . . whatever you want, so that they go without food without even realizing it.

Every time I hear Diego face social issues with this strength and with this clarity, I find myself asking him if he realizes how unusual it is for a footballer to express himself in these terms—almost like a politician. He shakes his head and laughs.

MARADONA: You know what, Gianni? During the last chat I had with Fidel, he also asked me: "Why don't you go into politics?" And I replied: "No, Fidel, I prefer to stay on the side of the people and not put my hands in their pockets." My life, which was deeply shaped by football, is for the people. I am for people. And if someone were to argue that I'm an idealist, or that I tell lies, I can only answer him in one way: I've always been like this. I've been fighting for more than thirty years against this state of affairs. And they couldn't bring me down, although, I assure you, they fired more missiles at me than at Saddam Hussein!

Based on these considerations, I guess Diego wasn't very surprised to discover that it was a young Santos player who has now moved to Barcelona, Neymar, to declare his bewilderment at the contradictions of his country and of the organizing committee of the Confederation Cup and the World Cup, while Pelé did not.

MARADONA: Of course not! Pelé never will. He will never do it because he is part of the "family," while Neymar is certainly experiencing the reality of the Brazilian people. Gianni, saying this, is like discovering hot water. Nobody is surprised if Neymar tells people that certain achievements are still missing, because the same happens in Argentina and in so many other countries. The redemption of Latin America has just begun. A gladiator like Chávez has passed, but there are still many things to be solved. If Neymar is telling the truth, and strengthens himself, believing in these things, then he will be a footballer serving the people, not the corrupt leaders.

As a former sports journalist, I decide to move the conversation to the football being [currently] played, and the technical qualities of the new champions, the so-called top players: Neymar, Messi, Cristiano Ronaldo, Balotelli . . . And Diego immediately gives me his personal ranking: Messi, Ronaldo, Neymar, Balotelli.

MARADONA: Messi is my absolute favorite. Ronaldo has incredible shots, but . . . Messi's game satisfies me more, because Messi is much more "electric," more awake with the ball; when he gets the ball he knows exactly what to do . . . Maybe the difference between Cristiano and Messi is how Cristiano hits the ball. The kick of Cristiano, Messi doesn't have, but Ronaldo doesn't have the footwork of Messi. Messi can easily dribble past five players in one quick movement and this Cristiano won't be able to ever do.

At this, I tell him, Messi is probably his heir. I still remember the semifinal in Mexico against Belgium, when Diego scored two goals by just using this particular talent.

MARADONA: Yes, I have done it many times, because I was small! You know, Gianni, I have a secret that makes me very proud: sometimes [my daughter] Giannina puts my nephew Benjamin in front of the TV and he asks to see Babu's goals. My goals. The first time I told her: "Come off it, Giannina!" But the second time I started to cry, because he really likes to see my goals! And it's not to make me happy! The last time I was at Giannina's, on the 16th of May for his birthday, Benjamin, who always has his iPad in hand that he takes everywhere, watching football at a certain point said to me: "Babu, let's see your goals?" And I realized everything they told me was true. "Wow! What a goal!" He would say to me. Four years old! And my tears were streaming, Gianni.

The emotional moments that his family offers him are many. The eldest daughter, Dalma, acts at the theater and seems to be very talented. Diego already confessed to me on another occasion that he went to see her and cried.

MARADONA: Yes, yes. I was hiding in a corner of the theater, which they had offered me. I can tell you that I think she has a "Maradonian" talent in the sense that when she acts, she pours her entire self into it. She makes people have fun, she keeps them in suspense, and I believe that this is the most important skill for an actor. In this case an actress, like she is.

She studied hard, and she never wanted us to interfere. She goes to London every year, for a month, to see all the theater performances in London. In short, she is prepared, the girl.

I ask him if in his opinion, his son-in-law [Sergio] Agüero, striker for Manchester City, is a "top player." He replies that he is, without doubt, a good player.

MARADONA: I'm not going to talk about him as a person: those are things only my daughter [Giannina] can evaluate. She gave me my grandson, and with my grandson I have everything you could want. As for their separation and their legal problems . . . my daughter will live on what I will give her throughout her life.

What I see clearly here is family pride.

MARADONA: Giannina will never need Agüero's money to live comfortably. Of course, I didn't expect their story to end so quickly, because I saw that they were fine together. I've been to see them twice, traveling from Dubai to London: it's an eight-hour flight. Little Benjamin kept repeating on the phone: "Babu, Babu, when are you coming?" And I've always been lucky: every time I went to London I found the sun, and him, and he sang: "The sun comes out because Babu came, hey, hey!" And all these things, Gianni, he did with me because his father Agüero was always busy, with many commitments. One day he made me climb up a gigantic tower. And I thought: "If I fall from up here, I'll break all my bones!" It was like a Christmas tree, but made of ropes. When we got home, Benjamin said to his father: "Babu went up to the top of the tower, which you have never done!" And I said to him, "Benjamin, okay, but I almost killed myself!" Of course, there was some competition between me and his father, but I didn't think it would all end like this. I believe he is an accomplished man, and my daughter is twenty-four, with a new home in Argentina I bought for her with Benjamin's kindergarten nearby. She allows his father to see him when he wants, and certainly my daughter will fall in love again with someone who will protect her, and she will continue to live her life!

The emotion with which Diego talks about his daughters and grandson leaves me with few words. I can only thank him, because not everyone has the ability and the courage to confess their own joys and their own bitterness. And speaking of bitterness, I decide to introduce the topic of the South African World Cup, where Diego coached the Argentine national team to the quarterfinals, which they had not reached for sixteen years. Still, the press pointed to him as the only reason for their defeat. Diego sees it differently.

MARADONA: I believe that football players win matches and football players lose them. But I still take responsibility for the defeat with Germany because, just as I liked to win, losing was a blow that I still remember bitterly. We had also practiced the day before playing without the ball for twenty minutes, we had tried the new man markings, we knew how and where [Thomas] Müller (their star) would be placed, we knew how they would play in extra time, where the number 8

(Özil) would be placed, the Central defender, etc . . . Yet Müller, who always positioned himself as a lone striker, scored on us after three minutes! We had one of our best marking him—Otamendi—but football is like this: one gets distracted and is done. And in a world championship, replaying the match in your head is very painful.

We knew Germany was very strong, but we had a team that could have won against them. The fact is that if you start the game by going 1–0, it will inevitably affect you.

Among the criticism that has been addressed to him there is also that of not having wanted to summon Javier Zanetti and Esteban Cambiasso, veterans of the triple-winning Inter Milan team.*

MARADONA [*laughs*]: Neither Zanetti nor Cambiasso could be part of my national team. Zanetti because I tried it and it went badly; Cambiasso is a matter of taste. I like players who play the ball forward to advance the play. Cambiasso is a good strategist but he likes to bring the ball back and restart (reset) the play. He is one of those players I don't like much, despite him being a great one. Zanetti promised a lot, but I tried him in the match against Paraguay and he didn't play well. That's all I can say. To complete the picture for Inter fans, after winning the Champions League, [Inter striker Diego] Milito arrived in decent shape, but when we landed in South Africa he lagged behind almost all the top picks, including Martin Palermo. You know what? I now understand

---

*   Internazionale, captained by Javier Zanetti and managed by Jose Mourinho, won the scudetto, the Italian Cup, and the Champions League in May 2010.

why [Inter manager] Mourinho left immediately [for Real Madrid] after that incredible year. Mourinho is smart and thought: "I'll squeeze them to the max and then I'll leave!"

And anyway, I want to say one thing about Inter: against Barcelona [in the second leg of the semifinal], [striker Samuel] Eto'o played the whole game as extra fullback. We must not forget it: because yes, Mourinho had a good team, but Barcelona attacked from the first minute until the ninety-third, and Inter wasn't able to enter the opponent's penalty area.

Then of course, Mourinho won the cup, and he won it well against Bayern, with Milito's goals. But the storm had already passed. The storm had passed and Cambiasso and Zanetti were now ready to move on to life after football because they would now have their Sunday, Wednesday and Friday's free from now on.

Diego also has very clear ideas about the real reasons for his firing, and he doesn't use half measures.

MARADONA: They got rid of me because the first traitor against me in the Argentinian national team was [Carlos] Bilardo. He had said that he would have left with me, instead he stayed. And he stayed because, together with [Julio] Grondona's* son, Humberto, he is part of a nefarious society. Grondona's son can't kick the ball, he doesn't understand anything about football, yet he is currently the coach of the [Argentina] under seventeen, nineteen, or twenty, I don't know exactly. And everything Bilardo gets, he splits with

---

* Julio Grondona led the Argentine Football Association (AFA) from 1979 until his death in 2014.

Humbertito. Bilardo became part of this "game." And he be-
trayed me. According to them, they got rid of me because he
didn't like the people I surrounded myself with. I can just say
that with my players I have always had a frank relationship
and that with all of them I have maintained great affection.
I remain serene because I created the team, I called up the
players, I trained them and, above all, I myself took charge of
the team. Me, not the journalists.

After having gone through thirty years of disputes, that never
seem to never end, I find it inevitable to talk about an un-
pleasant episode that happened a few days earlier, when Diego
went to the American consulate in Dubai to apply for a visa
for the United States, to take his nephew to Disney World.
And the visa was denied. Maradona tells me he doesn't know
the reason and I tell him that in my opinion the reasons can
be just one of two, and neither of them are exhilarating. The
first, that a few years ago he was addicted to cocaine: too bad
that the United States has ten million citizens with this problem. The second is that Diego has been and is a very good
friend of the bosses of progressive Latin Americans, from
Fidel Castro to Chávez, to Kirchner, who do not practice
policies convenient to the United States.

MARADONA: Yes, I believe that the latter is the strongest reason. Because for nine years (and my daughter is a witness) I
have not taken anything. I am clean. I started another life, a
life I like, that has given me the satisfaction of being able to
get up every morning and see Dalma and Giannina, to be
able to enjoy football, and to be a technician . . . It must be

for this then, because I'm a friend, I admit it, of Fidel Castro. I was a friend of Chávez, and also of Correa, the president of Ecuador, and Evo Morales, president of Bolivia.

In any case, if they don't want to give me the visa it's fine. It's enough that my grandson can go to a Disney park. I want to see his face, I want to enjoy his expressions, because he's naughty, a real little "bandit." It looks like the Americans think I'm either very important, or they're afraid of me! One of the two! I am not asking for a visa to work, because I already have a job. I am applying for a temporary visa to be able to have fun with my grandson, who is the joy of my life. This is why I say that they were mean, very mean. Cruel, actually. I am not talking about the American people, I speak of their rulers. Everybody knows who artfully creates wars and then sells weapons to those who have won. As they did with Saudi Arabia after the Gulf War, they left them with old weapons so when the war was over they would need to buy new weapons from them.

In short, it seems to me that the United States shouldn't look at me. I've already done my duty. I joined the queue with my grandson. I had twenty Pakistanis on one side and twenty Indians on the other. I went without any recommendations, like a normal citizen. They sent me first to room 7, then to room 1, then to room 6. A Spanish speaking official said that my visa had to go through the United States, and this and that . . . I wanted to smash everything . . . wait a second Benjamin . . . smash! Break everything. I don't need the United States and the United States doesn't need me. When they needed to, they gave me a visa to be in the 1994 World Cup. They said to Grondona: bring us Maradona and we give you the visa. And so it was. The World Cup was on. They then cooked up a positive test for ephedrine but only after all the tickets were sold out for the games I was playing in. At this point, when everything is sold, even the Rolling Stones are no longer needed!

From the refusal to grant him a visa, we come to another story, this time totally Italian, but much heavier. One of Diego's lawyers, Angelo Pisani, gave me a document addressed "To the Public Prosecutor's Office of the Court of Naples," from which I learned that the appeals brought forward by the [former Napoli] players Careca and Alemão, as well as by Napoli, rejecting the accusation of having evaded the tax authorities, was accepted with the ruling that Maradona was not responsible as are Careca and Alemoa. But there is more! The tax authorities still boast that Diego is guilty, a debtor who did not pay his taxes. However, it was judged not a crime for the others accused—Careca and Alemão. In other words, for the mere fact that Diego was not present in Italy but was in Argentina and did not file an appeal, it was decided, thirty years after the fact, that he owed forty million euros.

MARADONA: [*laughing*] If only I had them!

I ask him why he thinks all this is happening.

MARADONA: I don't know, Gianni. Maybe the one who is giving me the bill is someone I harmed in the past. But I haven't got the slightest idea, because when I left Italy, I left without taking a penny. The contract that [Napoli CEO Corrado] Ferlaino promised me . . . was never paid to me. With this logic, nothing can be collected at all. And here lies the absurdity! How can they get something from me that I have never collected? Apart from the fact that Napoli was due, as per contract, to pay me tax free.

Yet that time, when I arrived at Fiumicino airport [on February 23, 2013], thirty finance police guards in uniform showed up to hand me a single notification, as if Bin Laden had just arrived! Do you know why I find this so sad, Gianni? Because I somehow feel part of Italian football. I believe I have lived in the golden age of your football. The teams against which we played entertained the people. I wasn't there at the time of [Sandro] Mazzola, of [Gianni] Rivera, when they played a good football, but limited to two, three, or four teams. In my day, however, there were many more strong clubs and they were much more competitive, filling stadiums. I find it very sad that [Napoli's] stadium in Fuorigrotta has struggled over time to fill up again.

I ask him if the problem of international and Italian football lies in the fact that there are no players of the level of Maradona, Platini, Zico.

MARADONA: It's part of the problem, certainly. People wanted to see Gullit, they wanted to see Matthäus, see Careca, and wanted to see me. And in those days there was really a lot of tough competition: Sacchi's Milan was omnipotent, there was an Inter that always fought for the championship, a decent Roma, Juve who, after Platini tried to get back on its feet and was buying enough. There were many competitive teams.

But if you want to know what I think, the real fault lies

with the executives, who have not been able to keep the passion of football alive in the common man who goes to the stadium. The executives sold the ball and went on to toast with champagne. That's it! A typical case is [former Milan CEO] Galliani: let's call him by his name. I saw Galliani carrying Sacchi's bag. And then when I got back to Italy he was president of the league. We are in bad shape! It's unique that a guy who is a bag holder should become an executive! And if you tell me that he won credibility through the successes of Milan, I will tell you that Milan's successes belong to the Milan players. Galliani has nothing to do with it.

Let's talk a little about his experience in the Emirates, and about the fact that he was unable to express himself as coach with the same brilliance that he had as player.

MARADONA: To tell you the truth, Al-Wasl Sports Club have had a hard year; I came [in 2011] here to have an experience. I liked the country very much, I liked Dubai very much, and I stayed. We certainly didn't have the best team. The sheikh wanted us to reach the final of the Gulf Cup the first year. And I was happy, convinced that we would improve in the second year, but the second year was disastrous for Al-Wasl.

But what I was unable to achieve as coach, I achieved by being a representative for the United Arab Emirates in the world of sport. Today I work for the Dubai Council, which is the company that hired me as a sports ambassador, and I feel fulfilled. We are about to renew the contract and I am very happy, also because we might do a reality show with children from all over the emirates, to teach them football and about footballing coexistence. Above all, I still have this sport in mind, I still think as a coach, and the contract that binds me to the Dubai Council doesn't prevent me from agreeing to coach a team one day. If it hasn't happened yet, maybe it's because they fear my personality. Two or three federation presidents from different countries have come to talk to me, but in the end they're afraid of Maradona, of the player Maradona; because, I tell you, everything else is part of the past. In Al-Wasl I never missed out, not even when I had a fever. I haven't even missed one training session.

I observe that the only real film in which Maradona's life is told as it was, is the one by Emir Kusturica.

MARADONA: [*laughing*] He was crazy like me, so we got on well.

I know Diego is working on a book about his life.

MARADONA: Yes, it seems to me that the time has come to write the book that truly portrays me as I am. Transparent, direct and not for sale. They say that everything has a price. Well, here I point out to you that this person doesn't have one. When I entered the field, I gave it my everything. And also outside of the field: I was in Rome in 2008, and in Rome they treated me wonderfully, when I went for the la Partita del cuore [Match of the Heart]. In Milan they tell me: "Now we can finally admire you. Before we considered you an enemy, because we knew that come another Sunday, maybe Maradona's team would be next and destroy us." But that's what I'd like the officials of the Italian treasury to understand. They have cheaply and easily erased many years where, through how I played football, I gave everything I had inside me to the fans, especially joy. By doing this, they took football away from me and without football I am nothing.

WHAT WE TALK ABOUT WHEN WE TALK ABOUT LIONEL MESSI

INTERVIEWS BY DANIEL ARCUCCI
DUBAI
JANUARY 2014 AND 2016
TRANSLATED BY KEVIN BORTFELD

The response came from the gut, strong and sincere.

"Messi is different. He has an extra gear. He's brave. It's not to say others aren't, you know? But we spend so much time looking for a Maradona that we put the brakes on the kids out there. We slow kids down who've captured our eyes and hearts, but who've reached a ceiling. I feel that Messi has no ceiling yet, you know? I feel like Messi is the special one we've been waiting for."

The response came from Diego Armando Maradona's gut, strong and sincere, but not from yesterday, when his words would have been obvious, even opportunist. They came from nine years ago, when considering Lionel Messi the world's best footballer would have been a faraway notion.

It was 2005 and, in one of his many metamorphoses, Maradona had tuned up his body enough to rival that of his glory days. Seated at the head of the kitchen table of his father's house in Villa Devoto—where he stayed in those days, dedicating himself to hosting *La Noche del 10* for Canal Trece—he answered a question in a way that would ring true today: "Aren't we piling too much responsibility on Lionel Messi, proclaiming him the savior of the national team?"

Nearly a decade later, once again seated at the head of a kitchen table, but in a place as far from Villa Devoto as Dubai, the man whose body has endured as many transformations as the experiences he's lived, hears that same question again. So much has happened, even the unimaginable happened: He had him under his command as the manager of the national team. But his answer will never change.

ARCUCCI: You singled out Messi in 2005, when he was not yet Messi. What did you see in him?

MARADONA: His approach to the ball was unique; the speed he brought with him to face the Europeans was distinct. He didn't stop; he doesn't stop. That's why I say he likes the goal much more than me. I paused more in my game, more to create than to score goals. I guess he does, too, but I liked to make the number 9 the goal scorer. I had more vision of the pitch; he has more vision of the goal. I think that in a few years we will be talking about an even more complete Lío. Maybe with fewer goals but surely with more overall game. If he's reached a ceiling, it's because he can't score three goals in every game. But he's going to be a more complete player.

The years slow you down, but they also give you the experience to avoid unnecessary contact. You think about it more. You make more one-twos. Today he'll do seventy one-twos per match. Somewhere in the future he'll do thirty and be a more complete player, who comes back to look for the ball in the middle of the pitch, who takes free kicks, who switches the field. Today, I can tell that Lío's free kicks don't strike fear in anybody. They were scared of me. There were parts of the pitch where the goalkeepers knew I was going to look to score. But one-on-one, Lío finds a way around the keepers. He has the timing and mental speed to play it to the side, to fake one way or chip it over the top, which he does better than anyone.

Diego insists on calling him Lío and not Leo, which is the nickname for Lionel, and by now there is nothing that will make him change. Just as it seems he will not change the concept that Lío, Leo, or Messi still doesn't have a ceiling, as he said in that chat.

ARCUCCI: You reached your peak at twenty-five with the '86 national team and with Napoli. Messi is almost twenty-seven, and you sense he still has much more to give.

MARADONA: For sure. And a lot of that has to do with personality. He takes things much more in stride than I do. So mentally, when making decisions, Lío moves in slow-motion. For me, making decisions was a lightning bolt.

ARCUCCI: Wait, we need to clarify: Are you talking about how he plays or how he lives?

MARADONA: I'm talking about personality. Look, I say it because I knew him as a boy and I knew him as a player. Perhaps the difference is he makes decisions much faster on the pitch than off it. Off the pitch he does what he wants, too. But it's clear he leads a quieter life than mine, heh.

In a time when comparisons are used more to criticize than praise, the urge to compare Messi to Maradona tends to favor more the latter than the former. The Maradona extremist says, "How can they compare Diego, who brought the Brazilians and the English to their knees, with that boy who doesn't even know the national anthem enough to sing it?" The Messi devotee says, "How can they compare Leo, who is a professional and spends his time breaking records, with that fat druggie?"

Fortunately, there are open minds that allow for a more complex and reflective look. Minds like Italian manager Arrigo Sacchi, who had both "the fortune and misfortune," as he said, of meeting both as adversary—against Maradona, when he was in charge of Milan in Italy, and against Messi as manager of Real Madrid in Spain. He wrote and spoke of both, at the time: "They put on a show. To watch them is a joy even for their opponents. Maradona was a unique football artist twenty or thirty years ago. The game then relied more on the ability of an individual than on a basic idea and collective training. He could always create something out of nothing. He could have played for any team and made them special.

"Messi is a product of the times. He loves football and plays it with professionalism and enthusiasm. His enormous talent is less instinctive and more cultivated by years at a football academy. He connects masterfully with his team and within that beautiful orchestra he plays extraordinary chords. Messi uses the team's synergy to his advantage. Maradona was more autonomous and self-sufficient. Lionel, unlike Diego, has no side effects, but maybe he hasn't developed his personality yet. Messi is more respectful of the rules, more professional, less of a showman. But both, in their own way, love football. They both stand out in their eras and will leave an indelible mark among the greatest in the history of football."

MARADONA: Sacchi is right

ARCUCCI: In what?

MARADONA: In almost everything. Look, I had to assemble my team, while Lío came to a Barcelona superpower. But remember, he is not to blame for that. On the contrary. He joined that team and made a difference.

ARCUCCI: You made Napoli great. Could Leo do the same?

MARADONA: I don't think so. Because of personality. But I am sure that he enjoys playing football as much as I did. We are different kinds of rebels. I was rebellious on and off the pitch. I always say, and I maintain it, that I did more harm to myself than to others. But I always did what I felt like doing. Lío is not a rebel off the pitch, but he makes himself respected. For example, the captaincy has been very good for him. And I want to remind that neither Sabella nor Bilardo made him captain. I gave it to him first. I did that because I saw that he would get angry when they didn't pass it to him at training. This is his rebellion: to make his teammates know that they have to look for him.

ARCUCCI: And is this a form of leadership, too?

MARADONA: Of course. I believe he's the leader at PlayStation, too. In the clubhouse, they'll play thirty games, and the one who wins 16–14 is the best. On the pitch, Lío is a PlayStation player, and his teammates understand that they have to pass it to him to resolve things. I see him doing this and not, for example, going to fight with Grondona. Someone else will, but he'll find out everything. In other words, I don't see him as a leader that feels about Grondona how I did because it's just not how he is. I do see him showing his anger on the pitch. But I don't think he likes to win as much as I did. I don't believe so . . .

ARCUCCI: You don't see that killer instinct that Tata Martino recently spoke about, for instance?

MARADONA: No. I don't see it. But I do have the memory of South Africa, which means just as much. I can still hear it, and I don't think it'll ever leave me, the sound of Lío crying when we were knocked out by Germany. I went over to him and told him he was going to have many World Cups to avenge it. I said it from the heart. Everyone was thinking about going home, about flights. And there he was, face down, crying. That's something very powerful, something Argentines need to know when they say he doesn't feel the shirt, that he doesn't sing the anthem. Those who say that are idiots.

ARCUCCI: For many, that World Cup was a great chance lost to see Messi lift the cup. And it was your team.

MARADONA: Messi played an exceptional World Cup with me. Exceptional. And nobody said that. Why didn't he score a goal? He made MVPs out of all the goalkeepers.

ARCUCCI: But in the match against Germany . . .

MARADONA: I repeat it again: we did not get the game against Germany wrong.

ARCUCCI: No? Are you sure?

MARADONA: No. He had nothing left.

ARCUCCI: Everything seemed to indicate that his South Africa 2010 was your Mexico '86.

MARADONA: I repeat: for me, he played a wonderful World Cup. And thanks to his age and the experience he's gained over these years, I think this is the right World Cup for him. Even going out with an injury helps him. Otherwise, he wouldn't stop playing, because he always wants to play. Always. That's why I say I'm happy they gave Cristiano the Ballon d'Or, while Lío had the Ballon d'Or at halftime. He who paces himself better is going to win. And Lío has already done that.

ARCUCCI: You see him holding the cup at the Maracaná.

MARADONA: It could be, it could be . . . But the thing is that it's Brazil, right? And while we have drawn an easy group, the

World Cup is the World Cup when the spaces shrink, when the big teams show up. There's Spain, there's Germany, and there's Brazil, with a tremendous defense. When you think about Brazil's defense, six or seven names come to mind. When you think of their attack, only Neymar does. For Lío, it will be a character test, to get all the crying out of his heart. Brazil 2014 could be his grand revenge.

ARCUCCI: Does he need, as some say, to win the World Cup to be the best?

MARADONA: What? No! Messi doesn't need to win the World Cup to be the best footballer in the world. It has nothing to do with it. Don't confuse the two. Winning the World Cup would be fantastic for Argentina, fantastic for the fans, and fantastic for Lío. But a World Cup will not take away anything he's done to get where he is.

ARCUCCI: And where is he?

MARADONA: Among the best of the best.

ARCUCCI: Which are . . .

MARADONA: The ones that everyone says. Di Stéfano, Pelé, Cruyff. They put me in there. And him. Heh, three Argentines.

POSTSCRIPT: DUBAI, JANUARY 2016

It's two years later, Messi still has not lifted the World Cup trophy. But as Diego had divined, he didn't need that to be the best in the world.

With Messi winning another Ballon d'Or framed on his TV screen, watching the award ceremony in Zurich from his exile in Dubai, Diego treated himself to a game of comparisons, imagining how many Ballon d'Ors he might have won during his playing career, if non-European players were eligible to win the award.

MARADONA: Each one has their own place in the glory of the number 10 shirt. I had a lot of fun. I enjoyed it a lot. I don't have reason to envy Lío, who has it now. Just as I say that Riquelme was the best number 10 Boca has had, the Argentina team had and has number 10s that know how to wear the shirt.

And of the Ballons d'Or, when I played in Europe they weren't allowed to give it to a footballer who wasn't European. How many would I have won, huh? How many?

In '83, they gave it to that passionless Platini? I did good things in Barcelona. I had recovered from hepatitis and hadn't yet crossed paths with Vasco Goikoetxea. I could have beaten him. One. I get my first.

In '84, again to the Frenchman? I'll say no because I left Barcelona that year in the middle of a mess and after the fracture. I still have one, that's fine.

In '85, again to him? Hmmm. What's up, man, did you buy that? It's OK. I'll stick with one.

In '86, Belonov? Igor Belanov? In '86?!? Well, there's no doubt, right? The World Cup year with the Argentine national team, for those who've forgotten. I win. Two Ballons d'Or.

In '87, Gullit. And what about me, pal? Champion with Napoli! I won the championship with Napoli. And after becoming world champion. Three. Three Ballons d'Or.

In '88, Marco van Basten? That's fine, he won the Euro. But that was a great year for me. Fourth. Four Ballons d'Or.

In '89, van Basten again? We won UEFA with Napoli. Could have been my fifth already.

In '90, my friend Matthäus? It's true, they beat us to win the World Cup with Germany. But I won the scudetto with Napoli, and we were runners-up in the World Cup. Sixth Ballon d'Or.

In '91, Frenchman Jean-Pierre Papin? They were having a hard time finding Europeans, huh?

Afterwards, of course, a harsh suspension forced Diego to retire. But he came back. And he came back again, in the endless cycle of deaths and resurrections that was his career.

THE LAST INTERVIEW

INTERVIEW WITH JULIO CHIAPPETTA
CLARÍN
NOVEMBER 2020
TRANSLATED BY MARISSA COLON-MARGOLIES

It's a time of strict protocols for everyone. And Diego, who is an at-risk patient, has had to adapt to the rules the pandemic has imposed. Isolated in his house in [the Buenos Aires suburb] Brandsen, and in his only interview with Argentinian media, Maradona agreed to answer the questions that *Clarín* posed to him through his director of communications on the occasion of his birthday. Number 10 speaks about football and life.

The kid who was born and raised in Villa Fiorito, the boy who wore out his only pair of sneakers on a dirt field, the young man who started to dream when he began playing for [the junior team] Cebollitas, who trained in the prestigious school of Argentinos Juniors, and who got on a roller coaster he never could have imagined. The coach who'll always be a soccer player. The guy who'd trap a ball with his chest even if he were wearing a new suit. A man of contradictions. He of the perfect World Cup and of the doping scandals. He who made his life go "viral" before the concept even existed. He who was the principal protagonist, willingly or unwillingly, of a constant reality show. He who, a few times, almost wasn't able to dribble around death. The man in which all of these ingredients and many more coexist. Diego Armando Maradona turns sixty.

CHIAPPETTA: What are the best and worst things that have happened in your life? Do you regret anything?

MARADONA: I was and am very happy. Soccer gave me all I have, and more than I could have imagined. If I hadn't suffered from addiction, I could have played much more. But today, that's in the past; I'm well and what I feel most sorry about is that I don't have my parents with me anymore. I wish all the time for one more day with la Tota, but I know that she is proud of me in heaven, and that she was very happy.

CHIAPPETTA: Raise a glass for your birthday and make a wish for all Argentines.

MARADONA: My wish is that this pandemic ends as soon as possible, and that my Argentina can overcome this and move forward. I want all Argentines to be well, we have a beautiful country and I trust that our president can get us out of this moment. It pains me to see kids with nothing to eat; I know what it is like to go hungry; I know what it feels like in your stomach when you haven't eaten for several days and this shouldn't happen in my country. This is my wish, to see Argentinians happy, with work and eating every day.

CHIAPPETTA: The pandemic hit you close to home: your brother-in-law passed away, your sister Lili was affected, and you also had to take strict measures. Are you afraid of the coronavirus?

MARADONA: This is the worst thing that could have happened to us; I've never seen anything like it. And it is hitting Latin America even worse. I hope it ends soon; there are people that are not doing well; many people who have lost their jobs and struggle to have enough to eat. I trust Putin; I am sure that he will have a vaccine for this soon because it's already too much to bear.

CHIAPPETTA: Do you feel that people change their behavior when they get close to you, see you, or shake your hand and hug you?

MARADONA: I will always be eternally grateful to the people. Every day I am surprised by them, I will never ever forget what I experienced when I returned this time to Argentinian soccer. It exceeded what I imagined. Because I lived abroad for a long time and sometimes wondered if the people would keep loving me, if they would continue feeling the same way . . . When I walked onto Gimnasia's [the team Maradona was coaching] field the day of the presentation, I felt that the love of the people would never end.

CHIAPPETTA: What does an Argentinian athlete of any discipline have that makes them do the impossible in order to defend the colors of sky-blue and white?

MARADONA: We Argentinian athletes leave our country very early; we live abroad for a long time and we miss Argentina a lot. Because of this, when the national team calls you, you come even if you have to do so swimming. Because it makes you feel, once more, that you are home, defending the flag, and this is what makes us distinct.

CHIAPPETTA: What excites you about Argentinian sports?

MARADONA: Everything. I watch everything, and I follow every Argentine athlete wherever they are. Wherever the Argentinian flag is present, I'll always be cheering. When I see the face of an Argentinian athlete who wins, I feel happy. The other day I saw Peque (Diego Schwartzman) and Nadal play and I suffered more than Schwartzman.

CHIAPPETTA: How did you experience the Messi-Bartomeu-Barcelona situation? If you were in Messi's place, would you have done the same and slammed the door?

MARADONA: I knew that it was going to end badly and thought that Leo was going to go. The same thing happened to me. Barcelona isn't an easy club and Messi was there for many years and they did not treat him how he deserved. He gave them everything, brought them to the tallest heights, and one day he wanted to leave to have a change of scene and they said no. It isn't easy to slam the door; there's a contract, a very big club and the people who love you. In Naples I didn't do it.

CHIAPPETTA: Who is the better candidate to win the Copa Libertadores: River or Boca?

MARADONA: Boca is good; I like it. Miguel Russo strength-ened the team in the back and now a couple of players have joined that have raised the quality of the team. River has been working with Gallardo for a while now and this is im-portant; they know each [other] very well, but I have a lot of faith in Boca.

ACKNOWLEDGMENTS

This book could have never happened without the kindness and help of: Simon Kuper, Maria Laura Avignolo, Nestor Barreiro, Rex Gowar, Dani Arcucci, Allegra Donn, Kevin Bortfeld, Luigi Gentile, Tiziana Bello, Jeff Biggers, Christiano Presutti, Antonino D'Ambrosio, Giulia Zonca, Tommaso Pellizzari, and Marissa Colón-Margolies.

DIEGO MARADONA (1960-2020) was one of the world's greatest soccer players. Growing up in poverty on the outskirts of Buenos Aires, he caught the attention of clubs from a very early age, and by his mid-teens he was being spoken of as the next great thing in Argentine soccer. He made his professional debut for Argentinos Juniors just a few days before his sixteenth birthday. In 1981, he moved to Boca Juniors, the club he had supported from his youth. For years he was linked to a move to a big European club until, finally, in 1982 he moved to Barcelona for a record fee of $7.6 million. It was not a happy experience for him, and two years later he transferred to Napoli.

Maradona bewitched the city during his time there, identifying with its underdog status in Italy, and he was embraced as if he was a native son. His feats with Napoli—who had only won two cups in their history—are extraordinary: two *scudettos* (in 1987 and 1990), two runners-up to the *scudetto*, an Italian Cup, an Italian Super Cup, and the UEFA Cup. As John Foot observes in his definitive history of Italian soccer, *Calcio: A History of Italian Football* (2006), "[In Naples] thousands of babies were named Diego, or even Diega." To this day, Naples is festooned with murals of Maradona; he is venerated as a local saint. The San Paolo Stadium has been renamed the Stadio Diego Armando Maradona. At the same time, he led Argentina to victory over West Germany in the 1986 World Cup and again to the final in 1990, where they were defeated by West Germany.

After failing a drug test in March 1991, he was banned from playing the game globally for eighteen months. In September 1992, he left Napoli and joined Sevilla for two seasons. After that, he returned to Argentina and saw out the remainder of his career playing for Newell's Old Boys and Boca Juniors.

He retired from playing soccer in 1997. In 2000, he checked into a clinic in Havana, Cuba, to help him rehabilitate from his drug and alcohol addiction. He credited Fidel Castro for saving his life. That same year he was voted FIFA's Player of the Century. He was involved in efforts to form an international player's union and was a consistent critic of FIFA because of its corruption. As manager, he led Argentina to the quarterfinals for the 2010 World Cup in South Africa. He also managed clubs in the Middle East, and near the end of his life he managed Dorados de Sinaloa, a second-division Mexican club, followed by Gimnasia La Plata, of the Argentinian first division. He was also a TV broadcaster, hosting the show *La Noche del 10* in 2005. The Iglesia Maradoniana is a religion dedicated to him.

At his 2001 testimonial for Boca Juniors, he said, "Football is most beautiful and healthiest sport in the world, without the slightest doubt. If somebody makes a mistake, football need not pay for it. I made a mistake and I paid for it. But the ball, the ball does not stain." He died in his sleep on November 25, 2020, of cardiac arrest.

DANIEL ARCUCCI is a leading sports journalist in South America. He was born in Puan, Argentina. He spent many hundreds of hours talking to Maradona over the course of his life and career, and he has been described as the number one Maradona journalist, "the one who knows most about Diego." He co-wrote Maradona's books, *El Diego: The Autobiography* of the *World's Greatest Footballer* (2004) and *Touched by God: How We Won the Mexico '86 World Cup* (2016).

He worked for thirteen tears with *El Gráfico*, becoming its deputy director. Following that he joined Argentina's top newspaper *La Nation* as an editor, where he was in charge of all its sports coverage. He participated in Asif Kapadia's documentary *Diego Maradona* (2019) and in many other documentaries about Maradona. He currently works (and has been working for the past fifteen years) at *ESPN F90*, a daily TV show that covers and debates soccer in Argentina and South America. #Casa10 is a space in his house where he works and where he keeps his most precious memorabilia concerning Maradona. From there he regularly generates articles and footage from the life and times of Maradona. You can visit #Casa10 at daniarcucci.com or on Twitter: @daniarcucci

ROGER BENNETT is the founder of the Men in Blazers Media Network, which has become one of the most popular football platforms in the world. He hosts a slew of podcasts covering multiple leagues in the men's and women's games. His television show, *Men in Blazers*, appears on NBC's Peacock. He created the number one podcast series *American Fiasco* with WNYC Studios, and HBO's *Succession* and *Band of Brothers* podcasts. He is also the author of *(Re)born in the USA: An Englishman's Love Letter to His Chosen Home* (2021), which debuted at No. 1 on the *New York Times* Best Seller list.

BRUNO BERNARDI was a legend of Italian sports journalism who worked for *La Stampa*, the Turin newspaper, for over thirty years covering soccer. He was one of Maradona's favorite journalists in Italy, to the extent that he was invited to Maradona's wedding. When Bernardi died in May 2020, *La Stampa* noted in his obituary that he was the "only Italian journalist invited to the wedding of El Pibe de Oro. For him, who used to devour technique and tactics, that invitation rang like presidential praise, a testament of professional estimation."

HUMBERTO "TITO" BIONDI was the first journalist to interview Diego Maradona. He was a TV and radio journalist as well as journalism teacher. He died at the age of eighty in November 2020, five days after the death of Diego Maradona.

GUILLERMO BLANCO is a journalist from Buenos Aires who has worked for *El Mundo*, *La Calle*, *Crónica de la Tarde*, and the magazines *Goles* and *El Gráfico*. In Europe, he worked for the newspaper *Sport* and the magazine *Don Balón*, in Barcelona. He was Diego Maradona's press officer for several years. He is the author of the book *Maradona: L'uomo, Il Mito, Il Campione* (1986), which he wrote in Italy.

JULIO CHIAPPETTA is the former sports editor of *Clarín*, one of Argentina's leading newspapers. A friend of Maradona's, he conducted the last interview with him and was also the journalist who broke the news of Maradona's death to the world. He told the Madrid newspaper *Marca*, "We published it at 13:06 (17:06 in Spain). That's when I got on my knees and cried alone in front of the computer."

GABRIELA COCIFFI is the editorial director of Infobae. She is one of the most prominent journalists and editors in Argentina. On Maradona's fifty-third birthday, she tweeted: "Happy Birthday Diego, who I've loved and fought with for 30 years but was always there for me in my difficult moments." She has played a prominent role in a campaign to identify the remains of Argentinian soldiers who perished during in the 1982 Falklands/Malvinas War and were buried in unmarked graves.

REX GOWAR was born in Buenos Aires and brought up in Argentina, the son of English parents. He has been a River Plate fan since he was five years old. When he interviewed Diego Maradona in 1980, he was working on the Buenos Aires Herald as a sports editor, general news reporter and photographer. For many years, as a Reuters sports correspondent in Rome, Paris, London and Buenos Aires, he interviewed many of the biggest names in sport. He covered 10 consecutive World Cups following the Argentina team, including when they won the tournament in 1978 and 1986. He was the first reporter to put Maradona's "Hand of God" quote into English after Argentina's quarter-final victory against England. His first book was published in May 2022: *Pumas, a History of Argentine Rugby*.

GARY LINEKER is one of England's greatest goal scorers. He was a prolific striker for Leicester City, Everton, Barcelona, and Tottenham Hotspur. After retiring as a player, he has been a prominent sports broadcaster, hosting the BBC's Match of the Day since 1999.

GIANNI MINA is a journalist, writer, documentary director, and one of the most beloved personalities of Italian television, especially for his work for RAI TV. He has written many books and films; he is an expert on the sport and politics of Latin America, and he won the Golden Kamera award at the Berlin Film Festival in honor of his achievements as a filmmaker. His most recent book is an account of his life with Maradona: *Maradona: «Non sarò mai un uomo comune» Il calcio al tempo di Diego* (2021).

THE LAST INTERVIEW SERIES

JOAN DIDION: THE LAST INTERVIEW AND OTHER CONVERSATIONS

"I'm really tired of this angst business. It seems to me I'm as lively and cheerful as the next person. I laugh, I smile... but I write down what I see."

$17.99 / $23.99 CAN
978-1-68589-011-7
ebook: 978-1-68589-012-4

JANET MALCOLM: THE LAST INTERVIEW AND OTHER CONVERSATIONS

"I did not set out to write about betrayal, but by writing about journalism, and photography I kept bumping into it."

$17.99 / $23.99 CAN
978-1-61219-968-9
ebook: 978-1-68589-012-4

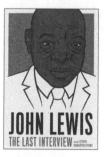

JOHN LEWIS: THE LAST INTERVIEW AND OTHER CONVERSATIONS

"Get in good trouble, necessary trouble, and help redeem the soul of America."

$16.99 / $22.99 CAN
978-1-61219-962-7
ebook: 978-1-61219-963-4

THE LAST INTERVIEW SERIES

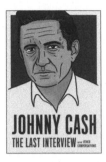

JOHNNY CASH: THE LAST INTERVIEW AND OTHER CONVERSATIONS

"I wouldn't let anybody influence me into thinking I was doing the wrong thing by singing about death, hell, and drugs. Cause I've always done that, and I always will."

$16.99 / $22.99 CAN
978-1-61219-893-4
ebook: 978-1-61219-894-1

FRED ROGERS: THE LAST INTERVIEW AND OTHER CONVERSATIONS

"I think one of the greatest gifts you can give anybody is the gift of your honest self."

$16.99 / $22.99 CAN
978-1-61219-895-8
ebook: 978-1-61219-896-5

SHIRLEY CHISHOLM: THE LAST INTERVIEW AND OTHER CONVERSATIONS

"All I can say is that I'm a shaker-upper. That's exactly what I am.

$16.99 / $22.99 CAN
978-1-61219-897-2
ebook: 978-1-61219-898-9

THE LAST INTERVIEW SERIES

RUTH BADER GINSBURG : THE LAST INTERVIEW AND OTHER CONVERSATIONS

"No one ever expected me to go to law school. I was supposed to be a high school teacher, or how else could I earn a living?"

$17.99 / $23.99 CAN
978-1-61219-919-1
ebook: 978-1-61219-920-7

MARILYN MONROE: THE LAST INTERVIEW AND OTHER CONVERSATIONS

"I'm so many people. They shock me sometimes.
I wish I was just me!"

$16.99 / $22.99 CAN
978-1-61219-877-4
ebook: 978-1-61219-878-1

FRIDA KAHLO: THE LAST INTERVIEW AND OTHER CONVERSATIONS

"The only thing I know is that I paint because I need to, and I paint always whatever passes through my head, without any other consideration."

$16.99 / $22.99 CAN
978-1-61219-875-0
ebook: 978-1-61219-876-7

THE LAST INTERVIEW SERIES

TONI MORRISON: THE LAST INTERVIEW AND OTHER CONVERSATIONS

"Knowledge is what's important, you know? Not the erasure, but the confrontation of it."

$16.99 / 22.99 CAN
978-1-61219-873-6
ebook: 978-1-61219-874-3

GRAHAM GREENE: THE LAST INTERVIEW AND OTHER CONVERSATIONS

"I think to exclude politics from a novel is to exclude a whole aspect of life."

$16.99 / 22.99 CAN
978-1-61219-814-9
ebook: 978-1-61219-815-6

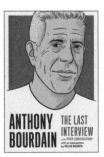

ANTHONY BOURDAIN: THE LAST INTERVIEW AND OTHER CONVERSATIONS

"We should feed our enemies Chicken McNuggets."

$17.99 / $23.99 CAN
978-1-61219-824-8
ebook: 978-1-61219-825-5

THE LAST INTERVIEW SERIES

URSULA K. LE GUIN: THE LAST INTERVIEW AND OTHER CONVERSATIONS

"Resistance and change often begin in art.
Very often in our art, the art of words."

$16.99 / $21.99 CAN
978-1-61219-779-1
ebook: 978-1-61219-780-7

PRINCE: THE LAST INTERVIEW AND OTHER CONVERSATIONS

"That's what you want. Transcendence.
When that happens—oh, boy."

$16.99 / $22.99 CAN
978-1-61219-745-6
ebook: 978-1-61219-746-3

JULIA CHILD: THE LAST INTERVIEW AND OTHER CONVERSATIONS

"I'm not a chef, I'm a teacher and a cook."

$16.99 / $22.99 CAN
978-1-61219-733-3
ebook: 978-1-61219-734-0

THE LAST INTERVIEW SERIES

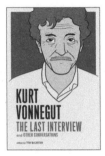

KURT VONNEGUT: THE LAST INTERVIEW

"I think it can be tremendously refreshing if a creator of literature has something on his mind other than the history of literature so far. Literature should not disappear up its own asshole, so to speak."

$15.95 / $17.95 CAN
978-1-61219-090-7
ebook: 978-1-61219-091-4

JACQUES DERRIDA: THE LAST INTERVIEW
LEARNING TO LIVE FINALLY

"I am at war with myself, it's true, you couldn't possibly know to what extent... I say contradictory things that are, we might say, in real tension; they are what construct me, make me live, and will make me die."

translated by PASCAL-ANNE BRAULT and MICHAEL NAAS

$15.95 / $17.95 CAN
978-1-61219-094-5
ebook: 978-1-61219-032-7

ROBERTO BOLAÑO: THE LAST INTERVIEW

"Posthumous: It sounds like the name of a Roman gladiator, an unconquered gladiator. At least that's what poor Posthumous would like to believe. It gives him courage."

translated by SYBIL PEREZ and others

$15.95 / $17.95 CAN
978-1-61219-095-2
ebook: 978-1-61219-033-4

THE LAST INTERVIEW SERIES

JORGE LUIS BORGES: THE LAST INTERVIEW

"Believe me: the benefits of blindness have been greatly exaggerated. If I could see, I would never leave the house, I'd stay indoors reading the many books that surround me."

translated by KIT MAUDE

$15.95 / $15.95 CAN
978-1-61219-204-8
ebook: 978-1-61219-205-5

HANNAH ARENDT: THE LAST INTERVIEW

"There are no dangerous thoughts for the simple reason that thinking itself is such a dangerous enterprise."

$15.95 / $15.95 CAN
978-1-61219-311-3
ebook: 978-1-61219-312-0

RAY BRADBURY: THE LAST INTERVIEW

"You don't have to destroy books to destroy a culture. Just get people to stop reading them."

$15.95 / $15.95 CAN
978-1-61219-421-9
ebook: 978-1-61219-422-6

THE LAST INTERVIEW SERIES

JAMES BALDWIN: THE LAST INTERVIEW

"You don't realize that you're intelligent
until it gets you into trouble."

$16.99 / $22.99 CAN
978-1-61219-400-4
ebook: 978-1-61219-401-1

GABRIEL GÁRCIA MÁRQUEZ: THE LAST INTERVIEW

"The only thing the Nobel Prize is good for is
not having to wait in line."

$15.95 / $15.95 CAN
978-1-61219-480-6
ebook: 978-1-61219-481-3

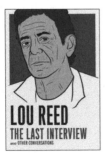

LOU REED: THE LAST INTERVIEW

"Hubert Selby. William Burroughs. Allen Ginsberg.
Delmore Schwartz... I thought if you could do what
those writers did and put it to drums and guitar,
you'd have the greatest thing on earth."

$15.95 / $15.95 CAN
978-1-61219-478-3
ebook: 978-1-61219-479-0

THE LAST INTERVIEW SERIES

ERNEST HEMINGWAY: THE LAST INTERVIEW

"The most essential gift for a good writer is a built-in, shockproof shit detector."

$15.95 / $20.95 CAN
978-1-61219-522-3
ebook: 978-1-61219-523-0

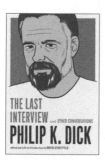

PHILIP K. DICK: THE LAST INTERVIEW

"The basic thing is, how frightened are you of chaos? And how happy are you with order?"

$15.95 / $20.95 CAN
978-1-61219-526-1
ebook: 978-1-61219-527-8

NORA EPHRON: THE LAST INTERVIEW

"You better *make* them care about what you think. It had better be quirky or perverse or thoughtful enough so that you hit some chord in them. Otherwise, it doesn't work."

$15.95 / $20.95 CAN
978-1-61219-524-7
ebook: 978-1-61219-525-4

THE LAST INTERVIEW SERIES

JANE JACOBS: THE LAST INTERVIEW

"I would like it to be understood that all our human economic achievements have been done by ordinary people, not by exceptionally educated people, or by elites, or by supernatural forces."

$15.95 / $20.95 CAN
978-1-61219-534-6
ebook: 978-1-61219-535-3

DAVID BOWIE: THE LAST INTERVIEW

"I have no time for glamour. It seems a ridiculous thing to strive for... A clean pair of shoes should serve quite well."

$16.99 / $22.99 CAN
978-1-61219-575-9
ebook: 978-1-61219-576-6

MARTIN LUTHER KING, JR.: THE LAST INTERVIEW

"Injustice anywhere is a threat to justice everywhere."

$15.99 / $21.99 CAN
978-1-61219-616-9
ebook: 978-1-61219-617-6